THE STEP BY STEP ART OF

Floral Paper Crafts

Published by
CHARTWELL BOOKS, INC.
A Division of **BOOK SALES, INC.**
110 Enterprise Avenue
Secaucus, New Jersey 07094

CLB 3330
© 1994 CLB Publishing Ltd,
Godalming, Surrey, England
Printed and bound in Singapore
ISBN 0-7858-0073-5

THE STEP BY STEP ART OF
Floral Paper Crafts

Text and Floral Designs by
CHERYL OWEN

Photography by
STEVE TANNER

CHARTWELL
BOOKS, INC.

Contents

Materials

Paper and card

There is a wonderful choice of paper and card available for craft use nowadays. Many art shops, stores and suppliers stock handmade, textured papers which, although often expensive, will make a handcrafted model extra special.

Soft, lightweight papers are suitable for making a wide variety of flowers. **Unryu** is a thin, Japanese paper textured with fine fibres. It is available in many colours and has been used to make many of the flowers in this book - for example, the white roses on page 35. **Mingei** is another Japanese paper that is soft to handle - see the tiger lilies and leaves on page 38 for an example of its use.

Crepe paper is a highly versatile paper. Interesting effects can be achieved since it will stretch when the grain is gently pulled apart. When cutting, match any arrow on the template to the grain on the crepe paper. Tissue paper has been used for flowers throughout the book. Although delicate, two layers can be spray-glued together to make it stronger and to add density. Tissue paper petals can be dampened to make them crinkle, or painted to achieve realistic petal colours. The sun will fade crepe paper and tissue paper, so take care not to display paper flowers in full sunlight.

Wood veneer paper is available from specialist paper suppliers, shops or stores and looks highly realistic. Sugar paper is inexpensive and widely available in a variety of colours. It is an ideal paper for painting and makes excellent foliage.

Most of the card used for projects in this book is thin and lightweight, similar to that used for making cereal packets. Since card does not fold easily, you will need to score along any designated folds with a craft knife so that it folds smoothly and accurately. Mounting board comes in a variety

of thicknesses, four-sheet and six-sheet thicknesses being the most versatile.

Craft accessories

Wire is needed in varying gauges of thickness. The wire gauges referred to are British Standard gauges; the higher the gauge number, the finer the wire. When a project suggests using thin wire, use 22 gauge wire which is 0.711 mm (0.028 in) thick or 24 gauge wire which is 0.0559 mm (0.022 in) thick. Use thin wire mostly for wiring flowers and leaves, and thick wire for stems. Use 18 gauge wire, which is 1.22 mm (0.048 in) thick, where thick wire is suggested. Wires come in standard lengths or on a reel from florist and craft suppliers.

__Bonsai wire__, available from garden centres, stores or suppliers, is thick but very pliable. Consequently, it makes good, strong stems.

__Covered wires__ are available in standard gauges from florists and craft shops or suppliers. The wire is covered with coloured paper - usually green - although other colours can be obtained.

__Stamen strings__ are short strings with solid, coloured ends which can be cut or folded in half to form short, stemmed stamens. They are inexpensive and can be bought in bundles at craft shops. There are many different types - round or pointed, matt or glossy, in a wide range of colours and sizes. Stamens can be coloured with paints or felt pens.

__Floral tape__, often known as __gutta-percha__, is available in a variety of colours from florists and florists' suppliers. It is a strong, flexible paper tape impregnated with a waxy substance that makes it self-adhesive. Use green tape for most projects.

__Cotton pulp__ or __polystyrene balls__ and __beads__, available from craft shops, stores and suppliers, can be painted or covered with paper and are useful for making flower centres, berries and miniature vegetables.

__Cotton wool__ is used to pad out flower centres and buds. Use yellow cotton wool if it is likely to be visible. Natural materials such as dried flowers, grasses and pine cones add texture and interest to a paper model. Wooden cocktail sticks are useful for making accessories.

Paints

Using the appropriate coloured paper can make all the difference in creating a handcrafted flower. If you do not have paper in a suitable colour, simply paint it. Several petals can be painted at one time by placing them on a plastic carrier bag that has been cut and laid open.

*Mix **Indian inks** to produce realistic floral colours. **Watercolour, acrylic** and **poster paints** are also useful. Craft paints are available in a range of glossy, pearlized, metallic and matt finishes. The colours are easy to mix and most are non-toxic.*

Equipment

Much of the equipment needed for floral paper crafts falls within the standard desk range. For comfort and safety, work on a flat, clean surface, taking care to keep sharp implements, glues and paints well out of the reach of children.

For drawing and cutting

*A **propelling pencil** or **sharpened HB pencil** is best for drawing. For accuracy always use a **ruler** and **set square** when drawing squares and rectangles. Draw circles with a **compass** or use a **circle stencil** for miniature circles.*

***Sharp, pointed scissors** are vital; a small pair is best for cutting detailed shapes. **Craft knives** give a neater cut on card; always use a cutting mat and replace blades often, since a blunt blade will tear. Use wire-cutters to cut wire and a **small hacksaw** to cut wooden dowelling.*

For sticking

Masking tape is a low-tack tape which does not dry out quickly. It can be used to hold paper and templates in position temporarily and later removed without marking the surface.

Always read the manufacturer's instructions for adhesives and test them on scrap paper before use. Check that glue does not seep to the surface on thin paper.

Generally, when sticking paper to paper, use a **latex glue**. When sticking card or paper to wire, use an **all-purpose household glue**. **PVA (polyvinyl acetate) medium** is a versatile, non-toxic adhesive used to make papier mâché.

Spray glue gives an even, professional finish but must be used in a well-ventilated room with the surrounding area protected with newspaper. Use spray glue when applying two layers of card or paper together. Always use spray glue that is free of CFCs.

Double-sided adhesive tape is a clean alternative to glue. The tape is adhesive on both sides with a backing tape that can be removed when ready for application.

For modelling and finishing

Use good quality **paintbrushes** for painting. A natural sponge can be used to dab on paint for a softened effect. Painted components can be mounted onto cocktail sticks or wire and inserted into **plastic clay** to dry. Plastic clay can also be modelled into moulds to make papier mâché.

Use a **thick needle**, an awl or **pointed scissors** tip to pierce holes in paper. A hole punch can be used to make larger holes. **Wooden dowelling** is available in various thicknesses and is useful for making stalks or constructing models. Balsa wood is very soft and easy to saw. Look for interesting branches and twigs that have been discarded; they are useful for stalks and ornamental tree trunks.

Dry foam oasis is a lightweight foam that is used for dried flower arrangements. It is available from florists, garden centres or suppliers in block form, balls and rings. Cut the foam with a knife.

Look for **unusual baskets** and **vases** for displaying your models. Decorate **willow rings** to hang on a wall or to form a table centrepiece. Containers for plants can be weighted with **quick-set cement**.

13

Techniques

The same basic techniques are involved in many of the projects. Before you start any design, carefully read the techniques described in this section. It is also helpful to study the photographs of finished projects and read through the step-by-step instructions that accompany each project before you begin.

Cutting petals

1 Layers of thin paper can be stapled together so that a number of copies of the same motif can be cut at one time.

Draw around the template on paper, roughly cut it out and staple it to layers of paper. Do not staple too many layers together or the cutting will be inaccurate; ten layers is sufficient for tissue paper. Cut out the motifs.

Curling petals

1 Petal and leaf edges can be curled by drawing the paper over a scissors blade. Take care not to handle delicate papers too firmly or they may tear.

Wired method

1 If the leaf you wish to wire has veins, fold along the veins by pinching the paper between thumb and finger. Use all-purpose household glue to stick a length of covered wire along the centre, with the wire extending below the base. If the glue tube has a narrow nozzle, insert the wire into the nozzle to distribute the glue evenly. Leave to dry, then bend the leaf into position.

Binding wire

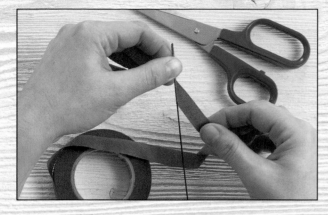

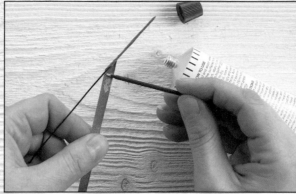

1 *Floral tape is used to cover wires and bind components together. It is 1 cm ($^3/_8$ in) wide and can be cut lengthways in half to make it easier to handle. Hold the tape diagonally under one end of the wire. Roll the wire into the tape, stretching the tape gently as you work. Cut off excess tape. If you are binding stamens or the base of a flower, dab the start of the tape with glue.*

2 *Wire can be bound with paper if you do not have a suitable coloured floral tape. Cut 5 mm ($^1/_4$ in) wide strips of paper and spread one end sparingly with glue using a cocktail stick. Hold the paper diagonally under one end of the wire. Roll the wire into the tape, applying more glue when necessary.*

Weighted method

1 *Quick-set cement is used to weight containers for paper plants. Cover the hole inside the container with masking tape. Following the manufacturer's instructions, pour the cement into the container and gradually stir in water. When the pot is three-quarters full, insert the plant stem or trunk upright in the centre. Add more cement until it reaches 1.5 cm ($^5/_8$ in) below the rim. Set aside to harden.*

Cutting and scoring

1 *Cover a flat, stable surface with a cutting mat or a piece of corrugated card. When cutting card with a craft knife, do not press too hard or cut all the way through at first; gradually cut deeper and deeper. Always cut crepe and tissue paper with scissors to avoid tearing. If scoring, do not cut all the way through the card but break the top surface only. Cut straight lines against a metal ruler.*

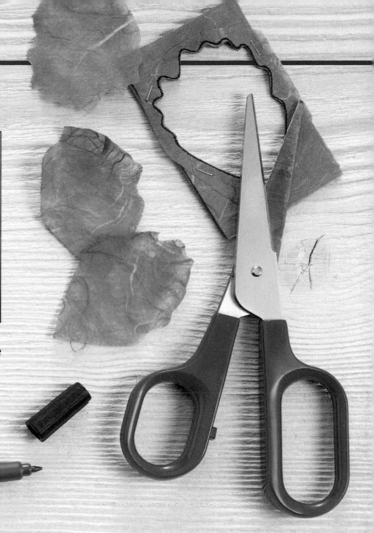

Full rose

1 Bend the end of a length of thin wire into a hook. Glue a piece of cotton wool around the hook.

2 Make the rose from crepe or soft, lightweight paper. Use the templates on page 92 to cut 1 rose centre, 4 small rose petals, 3 medium rose petals and 6 large rose petals from paper. If using crepe, cut the pieces with the arrow parallel to the grain of the paper. Pull the ends of the petals over a scissors blade to curl them. Gently pull crepe paper petals across the centre to stretch them. Glue the rose centre around the cotton wool to form a tube.

3 Apply glue to the base of the small petals and stick around the tube, overlapping the petals.

4 Add the medium petals, then the large ones, overlapping the petal edges. Squeeze the base of the petals to the wire.

5 Use the templates on page 92 to cut a set of sepals and 5 leaves from green paper. Pull the tips over a scissors blade to curl them backwards. Glue the sepals under the rose. Use green covered wire to make the leaves, following the wired method on page 14. Bind the leaf stems together and splay open the leaves. Bind the rose base and stem with floral tape, catching in the leaves below the rose.

Field poppy

1 Dab glue onto the end of a length of thick wire and insert into a cotton pulp ball 1.5 cm (⁵/₈ in) in diameter to form a pod. Paint the ball with green poster paint. Leave to dry, then paint a brown cross on the top.

2 Cut a strip of black tissue paper 11 x 2.5 cm (4¹/₄ x 1 in) for the stamens. Cut a fringe along one long edge. Cut the fringe ends diagonally to make points. Spread glue along the lower edge and bind the stamens around the pod.

3 Use the template on page 94 to cut 4 petals from bright red tissue paper. Dampen the petals with a paintbrush and leave to dry. Glue 2 petals each side of the pod. Glue on the other petals, overlapping the first. Bind the base of the poppy and wire with floral tape.

Peony

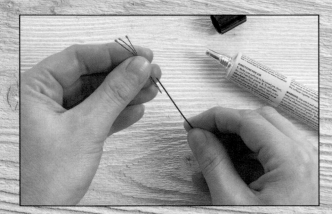  

1 Use the templates on page 101 to cut 1 set of sepals, 4 small petals and 5 large petals from fine paper or tissue paper. Cut one head off 3 stamen strings. Glue the strings to the end of a 5 cm (2 in) length of wire.

2 Pierce a hole through the centre of the sepals. Pull the points of the sepals and serrated edge of the petals smoothly over a scissors blade to curl them. Dab glue around the hole in the sepals, insert the wire through the hole and squeeze the sepals up around the stamens.

3 Glue the small petals, then the large ones, around the sepals. Bind the petals to the wire with floral tape.

Large daisy

1 Apply a thin film of bright yellow paint to an old plate. Dab at the paint with a damp natural sponge. Dab the paint onto lemon-coloured paper. Leave to dry, then cut a circle 4.5 cm (1³/4 in) in diameter.

2 Bend the end of an 8 cm (3¹/4 in) length of fine wire at a right angle. Cut a circle of card 2 cm (³/4 in) in diameter. Pierce a hole through the centre. Insert the bent end of the wire through the hole and glue to the card. Glue cotton wool to the card circle.

3 Cover the cotton wool with the sponged circle, gluing the circumference under the card circle. Use the template on page 95 to cut 2 large daisies from white paper. Pierce a hole through the centre. Pull the petal tips smoothly over a scissors blade to curl them backwards. Apply glue around the holes, insert the wire down through the holes and push the daisy up against the circle. Bind the wire with floral tape.

Eucalyptus

1 Branches of eucalyptus are simple to make, and look very effective. Use the templates on page 95 to cut small and large leaves from soft paper. You will need 4 small leaves for each spray; the number of large leaves needed depends on the length of wire used. Dab glue onto the tabs of 2 small leaves and stick to the end of a length of thick wire.

2 Glue a pair of small leaves each side of the wire 4 cm (1¹/2 in) below the first. Continue down the wire, gluing pairs of large leaves to the wire. Bind the wire with 5 mm (¹/4 in) wide floral tape or narrow strips of paper in a matching colour.

19

Freesia

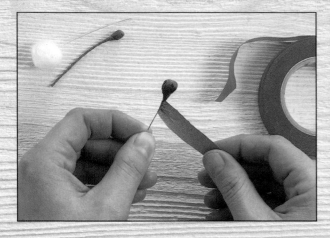

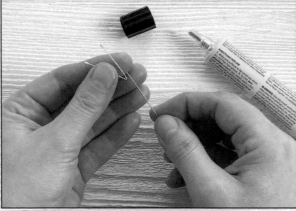

1 To make the closed buds, roll cotton wool into a small oval. Insert the end of a 5 cm (2 in) length of fine wire into the oval. Wrap the oval with floral tape and continue down the wire. Make 3 closed buds for each freesia - 1 small, 1 medium and 1 large sized bud.

2 To make an open bud, fold a yellow stamen string in half and glue the folded end to a 5 cm (2 in) length of fine wire.

3 Use the template on page 104 to cut 3 open bud petals from soft paper. Pull the rounded end of each petal smoothly over a scissors blade to curl it. Overlap the petals at the base and glue together.

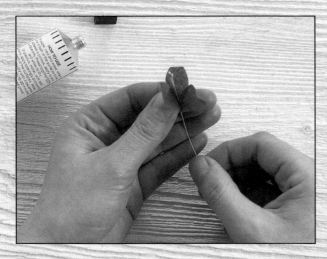

4 Wrap the petals around the stamens at the base and bind to the wire with floral tape.

5 To make a flower, fold 3 stamen strings in half and glue the folded ends to a 5 cm (2 in) length of fine wire. Use the template on page 104 to cut 6 freesia flower petals. Pull the rounded end of each petal over a scissors blade to curl it. Overlap 2 sets of 3 petals at the base and glue together. Place one set on top of the other, alternating the tips. Glue together at the base.

6 Glue the petals around the stamens at the base and bind to the wire with floral tape. Use floral tape to bind the smallest bud to the end of a length of thick wire. Add the medium-sized closed bud, then the largest closed one, followed by the open bud and the flower, all at 1.5 cm ($^5/8$ in) intervals along the wire. Bend the stem over at the flower, then bend the buds and flower upwards to shape the spray into a natural position.

Small daisy

1 *Bend the end of a length of fine wire into a hook. Glue a small ball of cotton wool to the hook. Cover with a circle of yellow paper 2.5 cm (1 in) in diameter.*

2 *Use the template on page 104 to cut a small daisy from soft white paper. Make a hole 4 mm (³/₁₆ in) in diameter through the centre. Dab glue around the hole, insert the wire through the hole and press the daisy against the yellow centre. Bind the flower base and wire with floral tape.*

Garden Delights

Keen gardeners will enjoy these pages inspired by ingenious garden themes. Use the ideas here to help you to make a model of part of your own garden in miniature or even to plan a new planting scheme. Capture the memory of your favourite spots in an attractive wall hanging to display indoors, or make yourself an indoor potting shed for 'gardening' on wet days.

Garden Delights

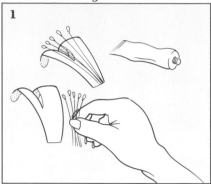

1 Use the templates on page 90 to cut 4 honeysuckle buds from cream paper and 4 flowers from yellow paper. Cut the heads off one end of 10 yellow stamen strings. Pull the strings and rounded ends of the buds and flowers over a scissors blade to curl them. Glue the stamen strings in bunches of 5 to the straight end of the flowers.

▼ *Trailing fronds of honeysuckle are displayed to great effect climbing this garden trellis.*

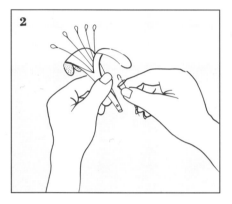

2 Wrap the long edges of the flowers around the strings and glue together. Pierce a hole 4 mm ($1/7$ in) above the lower end of the buds and flowers. Cut 6 cm ($2^1/_2$ in) lengths of fine wire, bend the ends into a hook and insert through the holes.

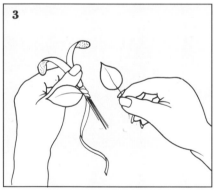

3 Use the templates on page 90 to cut 6 small, 4 medium and 2 large honeysuckle leaves from dark green paper. Apply to green covered wire using the wired method on page 14. Take a pair of buds and bind to 2 small leaves with 6 mm ($1/4$ in) wide floral tape. Bind the remaining buds to 2 small leaves in the same way.

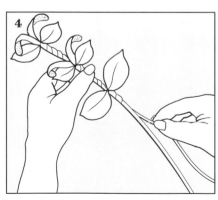

4 Bind 2 small leaves to one pair of flowers and 2 medium leaves to the other. Use 6 mm ($1/4$ in) wide floral tape to bind one set of buds to the end of a 24 cm ($9^1/2$ in) length of thick wire. Continue binding the wire, then at 3 cm ($1^1/4$ in) intervals add the other set of buds, a pair of medium leaves, the pair of flowers with small leaves, the pair of flowers with medium leaves and a pair of large leaves. Make about 18 fronds, varying the colours of the buds and flowers.

▲ *Bring the garden into your home with a novel trellis hung with vibrant clematis flowers.*

1 *Cut 2 large clematis flowers from white tissue using the template on page 90. Working outwards from the centre, paint the petals with carmine Indian ink. Leave to dry. Glue together at the centre, alternating the position of the petals. Apply 2 layers of yellow tissue together with spray glue. Cut 1 strip 12 x 2 cm (4³/4 x ³/4 in) and another 7 x 2.5 cm (2³/4 x 1 in). Cut a fringe along one long edge of each strip; carefully cut the fringe ends diagonally.*

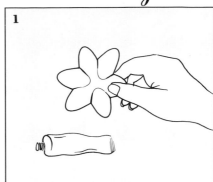

2 *Bend the end of an 11 cm (4¹/2 in) length of fine wire into a hook. Slip the hook between the fringes of the first strip at one end. Spread glue along the lower edges and wrap tightly around the hook. Pierce a hole through the flower centre; dab glue around the hole. Insert the wire through the hole and squeeze the flower around the stamens. Cut a leaf from green paper using the template on page 90. Apply to wire using the wired method on page 14. Bind the flower base and stem with floral tape, adding the leaf. Make about 18 flowers.*

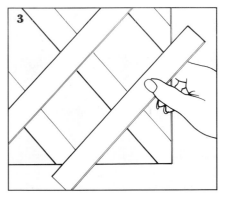

3 *Apply textured paper to a 59 x 42 cm (20¹/2 x 16¹/2 in) rectangle of mounting board with spray glue. Cut 3.5 cm (1¹/2 in) wide strips of mounting board and arrange on the covered board in a criss-cross pattern 7 cm (2³/4 in) apart. Cut ends level with the covered board edges.*

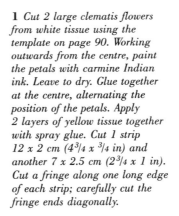

4 *Place strips along the edges of the covered board, overlapping the board by 6 mm (¹/4 in). Cut the ends level. Remove the strips and cover with wood veneer paper. Arrange in position and glue to the covered board along the outer edges. Slip flower stems behind the trellis.*

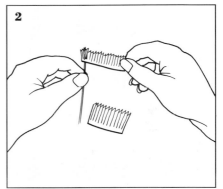

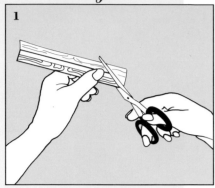

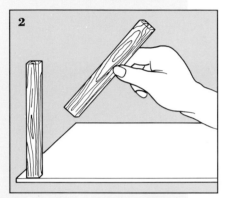

1 *Using spray glue, apply wood veneer paper to the sides, top and back of a box frame measuring 28.5 x 19 cm (11¹/₄ x 7¹/₂ in) and a textured stone effect paper to the base on the inside. Cut mounting board 17 x 4.2 cm (6³/₄ x 1⁵/₈ in) for the worktop; cover with red leatherette paper. Using the templates on page 91, cut a window sill, 4 legs, the window and door frames and 1 window division from mounting board. Cover the window sill with wood veneer paper, then cover the other pieces, trimming the paper level with the ends.*

2 *Glue the legs facing forward to the worktop under the 2 left-hand corners and 5 mm (¹/₄ in) in from the end of the right-hand corners. Glue inside the box frame against the left-hand wall and back wall.*

3 *Cut a 8.5 cm (3³/₈ in) square and 17.5 x 8 cm (6⁷/₈ x 3¹/₄ in) rectangle of a garden picture from a magazine. Glue to the back wall, positioning the square centrally above the worktop, the lower edge level with the worktop; and the rectangle 1.5 cm (⁵/₈ in) from the right-hand edge, the lower edge level with the floor. Cut acetate to match the square picture and glue the outer edge to the picture.*

4 *Glue the window sill and frames to the back wall over the picture edges and above the worktop. Glue the window division in the centre. Glue door frames to the back wall over the picture edges; the lower edges may need to be trimmed to fit the frame. Cut a rectangle of mounting board to fit inside the door frame for the door. Cover with wood veneer paper.*

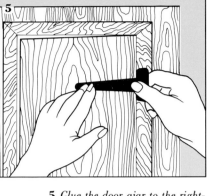

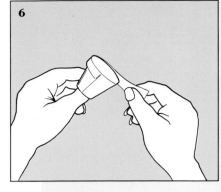

6 *Apply green sticky-backed plastic to both sides of sugar paper. Use the templates on page 91 to cut a bucket, then flowerpots from orange sugar paper. Overlap ends by 6 mm (¹/₄ in); glue together. Pierce holes on the bucket, insert wire through for a handle and bend back each end inside with pliers. Cut strips of orange paper; glue around the flowerpot rims.*

5 *Glue the door ajar to the right-hand door frame; wedge open while the glue dries. Spray black paper with metal effect spray paint. When dry, use the templates on page 91 to cut 2 hinges and a handle from the paper. Glue the hinges to the door and frame. Glue handle ends to the door, bowing the handle outwards. Follow step 9 on page 29 to make a trug and step 4 on page 56 to make a seed box.*

◀ *This finely detailed interior of a potting shed is constructed in a box frame that opens at the back, but you can adapt the instructions to a different sized front-opening frame. Arrange all the models inside the potting shed, adding some green netting and string.*

7 *Cut sugar paper for a sack 11 x 6.5 cm (4¹/₄ x 2⁵/₈ in), overlap ends and glue together. Staple lower edges together. Wedge a piece of oasis inside. Glue earth on top. Cut rectangles of flower pictures for seed packets. Cut fine twigs 6.5 (2⁵/₈ in) long for the broom, glue around a thicker twig and bind with thread. Refer to steps 2-3 on page 64 and step 7 on page 57 to make 8 onions and 3 tomatoes.*

8 *Plait lengths of straw, knotting the ends. Glue onions to the plait. Tie a tiny bunch of dried flowers with string. Insert screw eyes into the 'ceiling', tie on the plait and flowers. Use the template on page 91 to cut a trowel from silver card. Cut 2.5 cm (1 in) off one end of a wooden cocktail stick for a handle, paint blue.*

9 *Paint both sides of thin card green. When dry, cut a fork using the template on page 91 and a rectangle 2.5 x 2.2 cm (1 x ⁷/₈ in) for a shovel. Gently bend sides of the trowel and shovel upwards. Cut one pointed end off 2 wooden cocktail sticks for handles. Use a craft knife to cut a slit in the pointed ends of the handles. Insert the trowel, fork and shovel into the slits. Cut two 1.5 cm (⁵/₈ in) lengths of a wooden cocktail stick and glue handles to the top of the fork and shovel.*

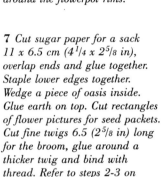

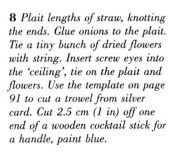

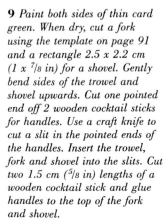

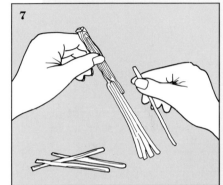

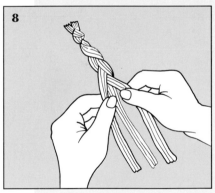

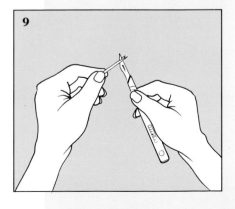

Garden Delights

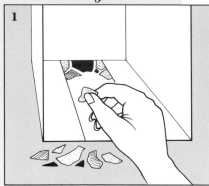

1 Cut one end off a shoebox; stand the box upright on the other end. If necessary, cut off the upper edges so that the box is 24 cm (9 in) tall. Cut the lid to fit the front of the box; cut an archway in the centre. Glue stone-effect paper to both sides of the front and inside and outside the box. Draw a path centrally on the base the width of the archway. Paint paper with stone-coloured craft paints; cut into crazy paving shapes and glue to the path.

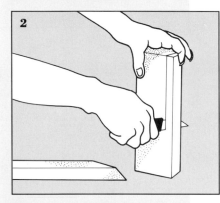

2 Cut two 2 cm (³/4 in) thick slices of oasis to fit each side of the path as flowerbeds. Cut the flowerbed edges that will border the path diagonally, cover with brown paper and glue in position. Insert a thick wire into a flowerbed against the back wall. Tape on wire 'branches' with masking tape. Remove the model and bind with brown floral tape. Glue against the back wall with some branches trailing over the side wall.

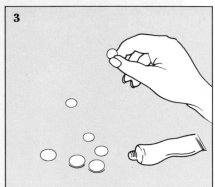

3 Cut small ivy leaves from dark green paper. Glue to the branches. To make daisies, cut 1 cm (³/8 in) diameter circles of coloured paper. Glue together in pairs at the centre. Snip circle edges, making a fringe.

▶ This enchanting walled garden has been constructed in a shoebox. A miniature trug with delicate cut flowers completes the scene.

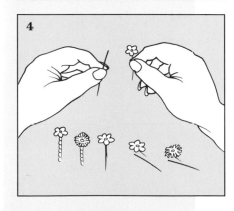

4 Use the template on page 104 to cut forget-me-knots from coloured paper to make into poppies. Pierce a hole through the centre of the daisies and poppies. Cut yellow or black stamen strings in half; insert through the hole. Dab glue around the hole on the underside. Glue string to thick wire and bind with floral tape. To make peonies, cut 2 cm (³/4 in) diameter circles of tissue. Glue together at the centre.

5 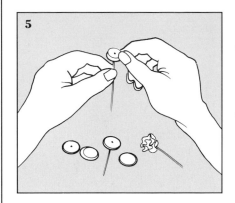 Pierce a hole through peony centre. Insert the end of a thick green covered wire through the hole. Dab glue on the end. Squeeze the circles up around the glue. Open out the circle edges. Cut 3 small leaves from green paper; glue under the flower.

6 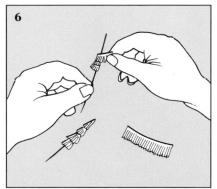 To make a red hot poker, cut yellow paper 3.5 x 1.2 cm (1½ x ½ in) and red paper 7 x 1.2 cm (2¾ x ½ in). Cut one long end in a fringe. Starting 3 cm (1¼ in) below the top, glue the yellow fringe around an 8.5 cm (3¼ in) length of thick green covered wire, spiralling the fringe upwards. Add the red fringe in the same way.

7 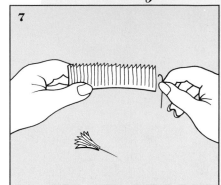 To make a fern, cut green paper 16 x 4.5 cm (6¼ x 1¾ in). Cut a fringe along one long edge; cut ends diagonally. Bend fine wire into a hook, and slip between the fringe at one end. Glue around the wire. Insert flowers, ferns and small dried flowers into the flowerbeds. Cut textured paper 3 x 1 cm (1¼ x ³⁄₈ in) and 4 x 1.5 cm (1½ x ⁵⁄₈ in) for bricks; cut curved corners. Glue small bricks around the archway, bending bricks in half. Glue front against flowerbeds.

8 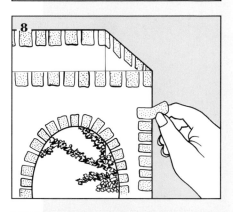 Glue large bricks over upper edge of the box and small bricks joining the front to the box sides. To make a birdbath, cut a 3.5 cm (1½ in) square of mounting board. Cut a 5 cm (2 in) length of 1 cm (³⁄₈ in) diameter wood dowelling. Glue a strip of fine corrugated card around the dowelling; glue upright on the square. Cut a section of cardboard egg carton 1.2 cm (½ in) high, cutting the upper edge in scallops. Glue on the column. Paint the birdbath grey.

9 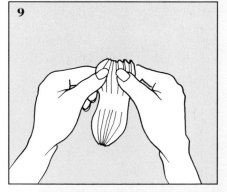 To make the trug, apply pine veneer paper then oak wood veneer paper back to back with spray glue. Use the template on page 91 to cut a trug from the pine paper. Cut the slits, overlap the ends and glue together. Cut the oak paper 18 cm x 6 mm (7 x ¼ in) and 12 cm x 6 mm (4¾ x ¼ in). Glue the long strip around the upper edge. Wrap the shorter strip over the trug as a handle; glue the ends under.

10 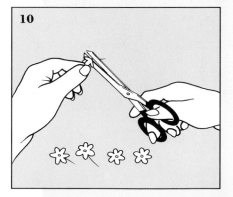 Make the clematis vines in the same way as the ivy branches. Glue to the front. Cut tiny green paper leaves; glue to branches. Spray-glue 2 layers of lilac tissue paper back to back and use the template on page 90 to cut tiny clematis flowers. Pierce a hole through the centre; insert half a yellow stamen string. Dab with glue on the underside. Cut string close to the flower. Glue to branches.

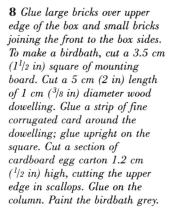

Garden Delights

1 *To make a template for the flowers, draw a 6 cm (2¹/₂ in) diameter circle on thin card. Cut out the circle, cutting a scalloped edge around the circumference. Use the template to cut the flowers from red and cream paper. Draw the flower centres with a fine gold pen.*

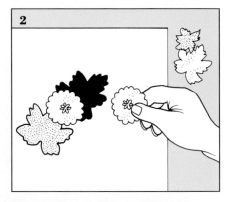

2 *Use the template on page 92 to cut chrysanthemum leaves from textured paper in shades of red. Arrange the flowers and leaves on golden giftwrap.*

3 *When you are happy with the design, glue in place with spray adhesive.*

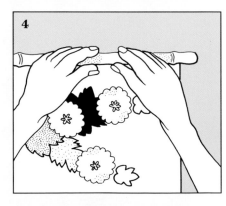

4 *Cut 2 lengths of bamboo 8 cm (3¹/₄ in) longer than the width of the wall hanging and paint gold. Leave to dry, then stick to the top and lower edge of the wall hanging with strong glue. Attach gold cord to the top bamboo.*

▶ *This stylized wall hanging inspired by a Japanese garden adds a feeling of tranquillity to a room setting.*

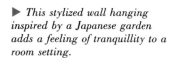

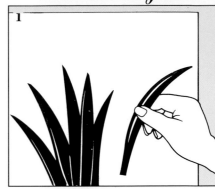

1 *Paint flock paper dark brown and leave to dry. Draw a simple design of bulrushes onto paper. Trace the design and cut out the pieces to use as templates. Cut the rushes from green paper, stems from beige paper and bulrushes from the flock paper. Position the pieces onto blue card. Glue in place.*

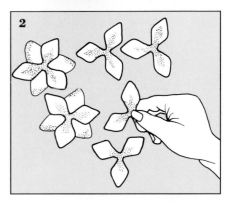

2 *Use the template on page 90 to cut 8 yellow paper large clematis flowers. Glue together in pairs, alternating petal positions.*

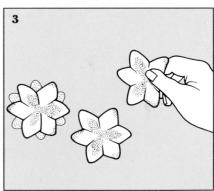

3 *Next, glue the sections together in pairs, alternating petal positions to form 2 flowers.*

4 *Cut fine slivers of orange paper as stamens. Glue to the flowers, radiating outwards from the centre. Glue the flowers to the picture.*

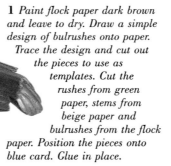

▲ *This bold collage depicting a quiet corner of a water garden is simple to make and would be delightful to give as a present.*

31

Beautiful Blooms

Re-create your favourite cut flowers to display in a vase or to make
into lavish everlasting floral arrangements. This way you
can select whatever blooms you wish to match your colour schemes,
even when they are out of season or difficult to obtain.
In addition, you can make bigger displays without it
costing the earth.

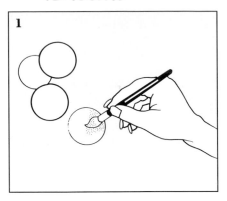

1 To make a delphinium spray, cut 28 white tissue paper circles 9 cm (3¹/2 in) in diameter. Mix together equal amounts of ultramarine, violet and white Indian inks; add more or less white if you prefer a lighter or darker shade of delphinium. Paint the paper. When dry, use the template on page 92 to cut 16 large and 12 small delphiniums.

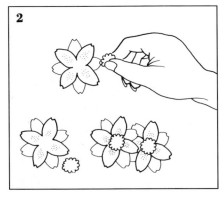

2 Cut 14 frills from white tissue using the template on page 92. Dampen with a paintbrush and leave to dry. Glue the centres of the large delphiniums together in pairs, alternating petal positions. Glue small delphiniums together in the same way. Glue a frill centrally on top of each flower; pierce a hole through the centre. Cut 28 black stamen strings in half. Cut fourteen 6 cm (2¹/4 in) lengths of fine wire. Glue 4 of the strings to the end of each wire.

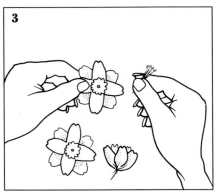

3 Dab glue around the hole of the delphiniums, insert the wire through the hole and squeeze the flower around the stamens. Bind the flower base and stem with 5 mm (¹/4 in) wide floral tape. Use the template on page 92 to cut a delphinium leaf from green paper; apply to wire following the wired method on page 14.

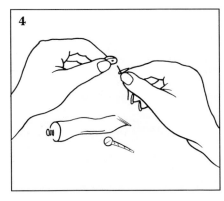

4 To make buds, roll 2 oval balls of floral tape 1 cm (³/8 in) long. Pierce a hole in the buds. Dab the end of two 5 cm (2 in) lengths of fine wire with glue and insert into the buds. Bind the wires with floral tape. Bind the wire ends to a 50 cm (20 in) length of bonsai wire. Bend the buds downwards. Continue binding the bonsai wire; add 2 small delphiniums 3 cm (1¹/4 in) below the top.

▲ *This vase of pale roses makes a classic display in any setting. It would add a welcoming touch to a guest room.*

◄ *Cool blues give a restful mood to a jug filled with delphiniums and scabious.*

5 *Add the remaining small delphiniums in pairs at 3 cm (1¹/₄ in) intervals. Next, add the large delphiniums in pairs at 4 cm (1¹/₂ in) intervals. Add the leaf about 8 cm (3¹/₄ in) below the last flowers.*

6 *For each scabious, cut 2 circles of white tissue 9 cm (3¹/₂ in) in diameter. Mix together equal amounts of ultramarine, violet and white Indian inks. Paint the circles working outwards from the centre. Leave to dry, then use the flower template on page 95 to cut a flower from each circle. Glue together at the centre, alternating petal positions. Use the template on page 95 to cut 1 scabious frill from white tissue; glue centrally on the scabious.*

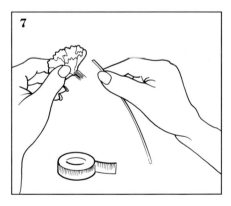

7 *Cut 28 large-headed cream or green stamen strings in half, bunch together, dab with glue and bind the strings with floral tape. If using cream stamens, dab them with green paint. Cut the hole in the flower centre, dab glue around the hole and insert the stamens. Glue, then bind, the strings to bonsai wire with floral tape. Use the template on page 95 to cut a set of sepals from green paper. Pull the tips over a scissors blade to curl them. Glue sepals under the scabious.*

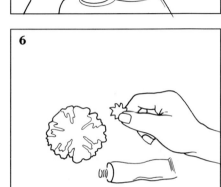

8 *Following instructions on pages 16-17, make full roses from soft white paper or pale apricot crepe paper. Use the template on page 104 to cut 5 ficus variegata leaves from cream paper. Paint the centre green. Apply 4 leaves to 5 cm (2 in) lengths of covered wire and 1 leaf to a 30 cm (12 in) length following the wired method on page 14. Bind the shorter wires to the long stem with floral tape.*

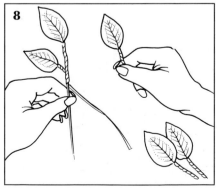

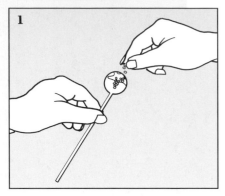

1 Dab glue on one end of 2 lengths of thick wire; insert into 3 cm (1^1/$_4$ in) diameter cotton pulp balls for a flower and a bud. Paint the flower ball with bronze craft paint. Dab PVA medium in a star shape on top of the ball and sprinkle on sesame seeds. Leave to dry, then shake off the excess. Paint the seeds brown.

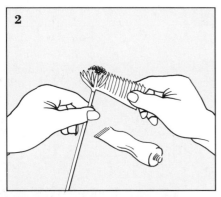

2 Cut a strip of dark brown paper 15 x 6 cm (6 x 2^1/$_2$ in) for stamens. Cut a fringe along one long edge and wrap around the top of the wire so that the stamens encircle the ball. Use the template on page 93 to cut 10 petals from soft mauve paper; a handmade paper was used for these poppies.

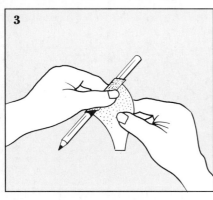

3 To curl the petals, wrap the edges around a pencil. Glue the straight edge of 5 petals to the top of the wire, then add the other petals. Use the template on page 93 to cut a set of sepals and 1 leaf from green paper. Glue the sepals around the base of the flower. Wrap the tips around a pencil to curl them outwards.

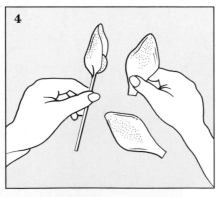

4 Apply the leaf to green covered wire using the wired method on page 14. To make a bud, cut 3 giant poppy petals; glue around the bud ball, overlapping the edges of the petals. Use the template on page 93 to cut a giant poppy bud sepal from green paper; glue to the bud, sticking the straight end to the wire. Starting at the flower, bind the flower stem with a 6 mm (^{1}/$_4$ in) wide strip of green paper, gluing in place. Add the leaf and bud 12 cm (4^1/$_4$ in) below the flower.

▲ *Fill a small basket with vibrant anemones or make the flowers in pastel shades for a calming effect.*

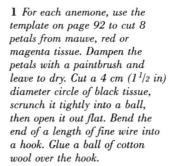

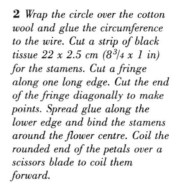

◄ *These giant poppies add a touch of grandeur to any occasion.*

1 *For each anemone, use the template on page 92 to cut 8 petals from mauve, red or magenta tissue. Dampen the petals with a paintbrush and leave to dry. Cut a 4 cm (1¹/₂ in) diameter circle of black tissue, scrunch it tightly into a ball, then open it out flat. Bend the end of a length of fine wire into a hook. Glue a ball of cotton wool over the hook.*

2 *Wrap the circle over the cotton wool and glue the circumference to the wire. Cut a strip of black tissue 22 x 2.5 cm (8³/₄ x 1 in) for the stamens. Cut a fringe along one long edge. Cut the end of the fringe diagonally to make points. Spread glue along the lower edge and bind the stamens around the flower centre. Coil the rounded end of the petals over a scissors blade to coil them forward.*

3 *Glue 4 petals around the flower centre with the coiled edge facing inwards. Add the remaining petals between the first petals. Bind the base of the flower and wire with 6 mm (1/4 in) wide floral tape. Glue piece of oasis into the basket. Make enough anemones to fill the basket, and insert into the oasis.*

4 *To make some foliage, cut strips of green paper 12 x 5 cm (4³/₄ x 2 in). Cut a fringe along one long edge. Cut the fringe ends diagonally to make points. Bend a length of fine wire into a hook and hook between the fringes at one end. Spread glue along the lower edge and bind around the wire. Bind the base and wire with 6 mm (¹/₄ in) wide floral tape. Arrange the foliage amongst the flowers.*

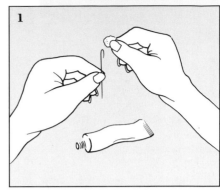

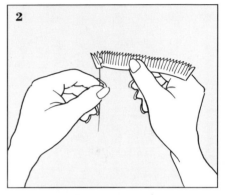

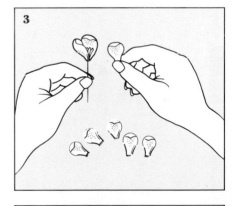

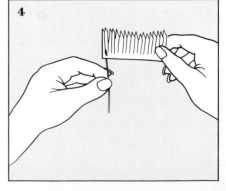

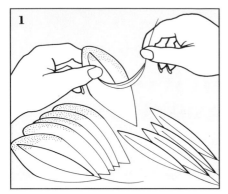

1 *To make a spray, cut 12 petals and 12 spines from orange paper using the templates on page 93. Glue an 18 cm (7 in) length of fine wire to the spines, with the wire extending at one end. Glue the spines centrally to the petals. Dot the lower half of the petals with a brown pen.*

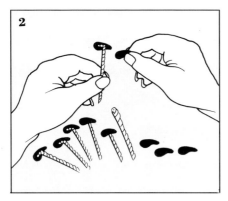

2 *To make 2 pistils and 12 stamens, bind fourteen 8 cm (3 1/4 in) lengths of fine wire with narrow strips of orange paper. Bind one end of 2 of the lengths of wire thickly, making them bulbous. Dot the bulbous end with a brown pen - these will be the pistils. Use the template on page 93 to cut 24 stamen heads from brown card. Bend one end of the stamen wires at right angles; glue to 12 stamen heads. Glue the remaining heads on top, enclosing the wire.*

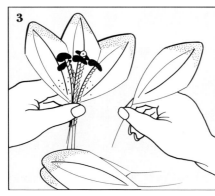

3 *Bunch 6 stamens around each pistil. Arrange 6 petals around the stamens. Bind the flower base and wires with a narrow strip of green paper. Use the templates on page 93 to cut 4 leaves, 4 large buds and 8 small buds from green paper. Apply the leaves to wire using the wired method on page 14.*

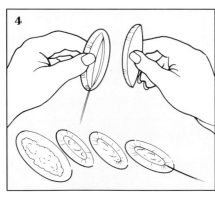

4 *To make 1 large and 2 small buds, glue cotton wool to each section. Fold 6 mm (1/4 in) up around the outer edges. Cut three 12.5 cm (5 in) lengths of fine wire and glue to an end of 1 large and 2 small buds. Glue the folded edges of a wired bud to the folded edges of 2 buds of the same size. Glue to the remaining bud sections. Bind the bud bases and wires with narrow strips of green paper. Bind one flower to the end of a length of thick wire with a narrow strip of green paper. Add buds, then the other flower, then the leaves.*

1 *Cut a 10 cm (4 in) diameter circle of card. Pierce a hole through the centre. Bend the end of a length of bonsai wire at right angles, insert the bent end through the hole and glue to the top of the circle. Glue a layer of cotton wool or toy filling on top, about 1.5 cm (⁵/₈ in) thick.*

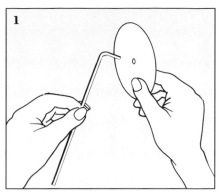

2 *Cut a 14 cm (5¹/₂ in) diameter circle of velvet or paper kitchen towel. Paint brown and leave to dry. Place the flower centre face down centrally on the circle. Snip the circle around the flower centre and glue the snipped edge to the back of the card circle. Cut a strip of yellow paper 70 x8 cm (28 x 3¹/₄ in), divide widthways into twenty eight 2.5 cm (1 in) sections. Cut each section into a pointed petal, cutting to 1.5 cm (⁵/₈ in) above the long edge.*

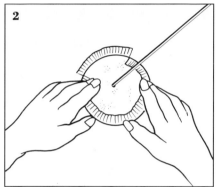

3 *Divide the back of the flower centre into quarters. Glue the long edge of the petals to the circumference, scrunching up the long edge to fit 7 petals into each quarter. Use the templates on page 94 to cut a calyx and leaf from green paper. Squeeze the petals up around the flower centre. Pull the petal and calyx tips over a scissors blade to curl them backwards.*

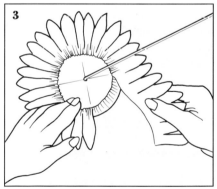

4 *Pierce a hole through the centre of the calyx, insert the wire through the hole and glue the calyx to the underside of the flower. Apply the leaf to wire using the wired method on page 14. Bind the stem with floral tape, catching in the leaf 15 cm (6 in) below the flower. Bend the flower head forward.*

▲ *These stunning sunflowers will be the focus of attention wherever they are placed.*

Beautiful Blooms

1

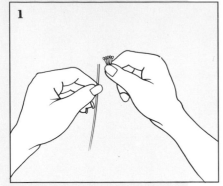

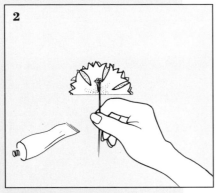

1 *Glue oasis in a basket and insert dried grasses, placing shorter grasses closer to the front. Make field poppies and small daisies following the instructions on pages 17 and 18. To make a cornflower, cut five 7 cm (2³/4 in) diameter circles from white tissue. Mix together equal amounts of ultramarine and violet Indian inks; add a little white. Paint the circles, working outwards from the centre. Cut 5 black stamen strings in half. Glue to the end of a length of fine wire.*

2 *Use the template on page 94 to cut 5 cornflowers from the painted circles. Fold 1 flower in half so that the petals lie alternately. Place the stamens centrally on the flower; dab with glue. Wrap the flower around the stamens.*

▲ *Trim a doll's hat with colourful flowers to hang on the wall of a child's bedroom. Make a large daisy following the instructions on page 18, and cornflowers from red paper following the instructions in steps 1-3. Glue to hat. Highlight with harebells and yellow cornflowers using only 1 set of petals.*

3 *Pierce a hole through the centre of the remaining flowers. Dab glue around the hole, insert the wire through each hole and push the pieces up against the first flower. Bind the base of the flower and stem with 6 mm (¹/₄ in) wide floral tape.*

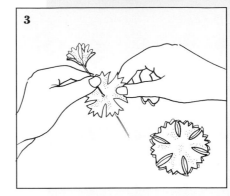

4 *To make a harebell, mix together equal amounts of ultramarine, violet and white Indian ink. Paint a piece of white tissue and leave to dry. Use the template on page 94 to cut a harebell. Pull the tips over a scissors blade to curl them outwards. Wrap the harebell around a pencil point, carefully overlapping the edges by 2 mm (¹/₁₆ in) and glue together forming a cone. Cut a lilac stamen string in half, dot the head with green paint and insert through the harebell.*

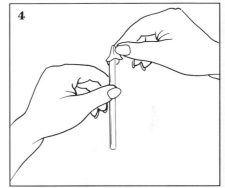

5 *Dot the underside of the flower with glue. Glue stamen strings to fine wire. Bend over one end of four 3 cm (1¹/₄ in) lengths of green covered wire.*

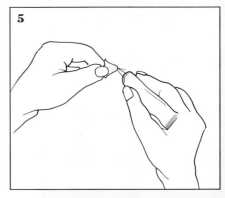

6 *Glue the wires around the harebell. Bind to stem with floral tape. Arrange the flowers amongst the grasses.*

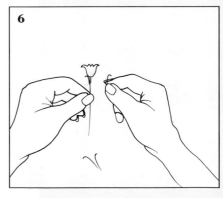

◄ *Evoke the beauty of a summer meadow with a basket of wild flowers nestling among dried grasses.*

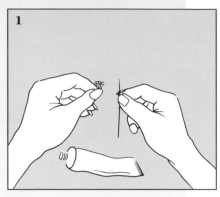

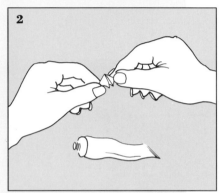

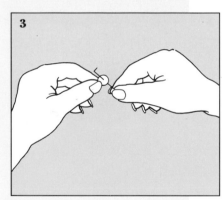

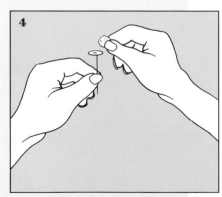

1 *Follow instructions on page 18 to make 5 large daisies and steps 6-7 on page 35 to make 5 scabious. For each lavatera, cut a 10 cm (4 in) diameter circle from white tissue. Paint the circle with a mixture of white Indian ink with a little carmine and violet. Leave to dry, then use the template on page 94 to cut 1 lavatera. Fold 5 yellow stamen strings in half and glue to a 7 cm (2³/₄ in) length of fine wire.*

2 *Mix together carmine and violet Indian inks and paint the stamen heads and fine veins on the petals. Pierce a hole through the centre; dab glue around the hole. Insert the wire through the hole and squeeze the petals around the stamens. Use the template on page 94 to cut 1 set of lavatera sepals from green paper. Overlap the end points and glue together forming a cone. Dab glue inside the cone; insert the wire through the sepals with points positioned between the petals.. Bind the flower base and wire with floral wire.*

3 *To make a marigold, apply a thin film of brown paint to an old plate. Dab at the paint with a damp sponge, then dab the paint onto orange paper. Leave to dry, then cut 2.5 cm (1 in) diameter circles. Bend the end of an 8 cm (3¹/₄ in) length of fine wire at a right angle. Cut a 1 cm (³/₈ in) diameter circle of card. Pierce a hole through the centre of the card. Insert the bent end of wire through the hole and glue to the card.*

4 *Glue cotton wool to the card circle; cover with the sponged circle. Use the template on page 95 to cut 2 marigolds from orange paper. Pierce a hole through the centres.*

◀ *Pretty summer flowers are displayed to great effect among dried sea lavender and vibrant green foliage on this colourful wreath.*

▲ *A charming wreath of winter foliage and Christmas roses makes a warm and welcoming decoration when hung on the door during the festive season.*

1 *Apply glue around the holes, insert wire through the holes and push the marigolds up against the flower centre. Cut ivy and peony leaves from watercolour paper using the templates on pages 97 and 95. Paint with green watercolours; paint the veins. Leave to dry, then coat with gloss varnish. Fix to wires using the wired method on page 14. Insert the leaves and bunches of sea lavender into an oasis ring.*

2 *To make a Christmas rose for the winter wreath, paint white tissue with cream craft paint. Leave to dry, then use the template on page 95 to cut 5 petals. Cut 16 yellow stamen strings in half and glue to a length of fine wire. Glue the petals around the stamens. Splay the stamens open. Bind the flower base and stem with 6 mm (^{1}/4 in) wide floral tape. Make 3 flowers.*

3 *Make 3 stems of eucalyptus following the instructions on page 19. Cut 5 ivy leaves from watercolour paper using the templates on page 97. Paint with green watercolours. Leave to dry, then coat with gloss varnish. Fix to wires following the wired method on page 14.*

4 *Bunch together the roses, eucalyptus and ivy and fasten with masking tape. Tie wired ribbon in a bow around the tape. Bind a willow wreath with wired ribbon, gluing the ends in place on the back of the wreath. Glue the spray of roses and foliage to the wreath.*

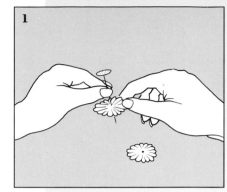

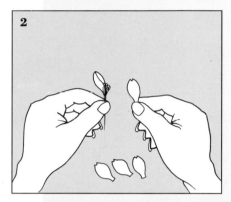

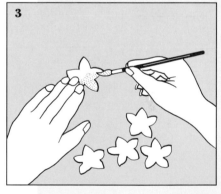

Potted Plants

Brighten your home with pretty plants that will continue
to bloom throughout the year and will never need to be watered.
Make a winter flowering Jasmine, for example, which will still
be flowering in the summer. There is even a stylish Christmas tree
for the festive season and some special
Spring arrangements for Easter.

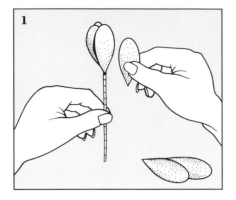

1 *Apply 2 layers of pink tissue together with spray glue, then use the template on page 104 to cut 5 freesia flower petals for each flower or bud. Bind an 18 cm (7 in) length of bonsai wire with pale green floral tape. Glue the pointed ends of the petals to the end of the wire.*

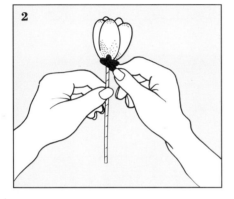

2 *Use the template on page 95 to cut a set of sepals from dark green paper. Glue the sepals around the wire, covering the petal points and overlapping the end sepals.*

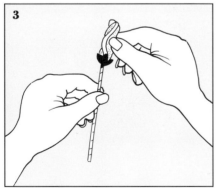

3 *To form a bud, overlap each petal two-thirds over the next. Glue the petals in place, then roll the petals into a tube and glue together. To form a flower, pull the petals over a scissors blade just above the sepals to bend the petals backwards. Bend the flower or bud downwards. The flower petals can be held in place with masking tape. Remove the tape after a few hours.*

▶ *Here are the ultimate easy-care pot plants. Fill colourful storage tins with cheery cyclamen and polyanthus plants.*

4 *Use the templates on page 95 to cut leaves from dark green paper. Paint the veins with green craft paint. Mix silver and green craft paints together and paint the details. Leave to dry, then apply to wire covered with pale green floral tape using the wired method on page 14. Do not fold along the veins.*

1 *Use the template on page 96 to cut 24 polyanthus petals from white crepe paper, matching the arrow to the grain of the paper. Gently stretch the upper edges. Paint the stalks yellow and petals mauve or red. Leave to dry. Overlap stalks of 6 petals by 1 mm (¹/₁₆ in) and glue together.*

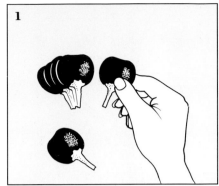

2 *Paint 1 cm (³/₈ in) of the end of four 11 cm (4¹/₂ in) lengths of thick wire yellow. Leave to dry, then glue the stalks around the painted end. Bend petals outwards. Bind flower base and wire with floral tape.*

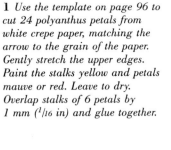

3 *Use the template on page 96 to cut 8 polyanthus leaves from pale green textured paper. Paint bright green with craft paint, leaving a tapering strip along the centre free of paint. Apply green covered wire to the leaves using the wired method on page 14.*

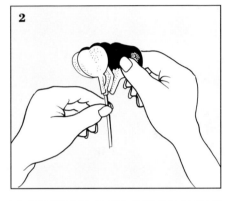

4 *Fill your chosen containers with quick-set cement and insert cyclamen flowers and buds and polyanthus flowers in the centre, with leaves positioned around them using the weighted method on page 15. Paint the cement brown when it has hardened. Bend the leaves outwards.*

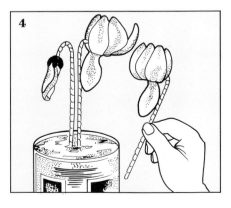

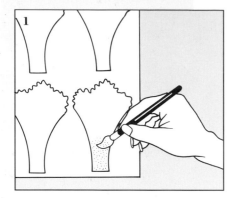

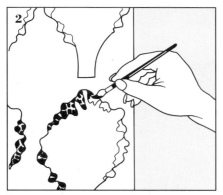

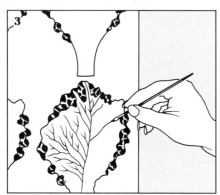

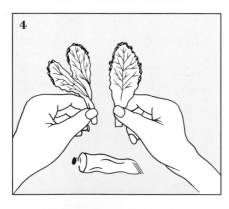

1 Use the templates on pages 96–97 to draw 6 of ornamental cabbage leaves A, B and C on cream sugar paper. Paint the leaves with a watery solution of green poster paint, using a lighter shade on leaf C. Before the paint dries, dab a watery solution of mauve paint on the tips. Leave to dry, then paint the veins using mauve paint and a fine paintbrush. Leave to dry. Cut out leaf A and paint the back of the leaves in the same way.

2 Use the templates on page 96 to draw 7 of leaf D and 8 of leaf E on the sugar paper. Refer to the templates and paint the green areas with a watery solution of light green paint. Leave to dry, then paint these areas in a darker green shade in a random patchwork pattern.

3 Paint the unpainted areas of leaf D with a very watery solution of mauve paint. Refer to the templates to paint the veins, using mauve paint and a fine paintbrush. Leave to dry, then use a thicker brush to paint along the veins with a watery solution of mauve paint. Leave to dry, then paint the back of leaves B, C, D and E green.

4 Cut out the leaves. Pull each leaf smoothly over a scissors blade to curl the leaves backwards. Roll 1 leaf A lengthways around a pencil. Remove the pencil and dab glue on the 'stalk'. Squeeze the stalk at the base to hold the shape. Glue the stalks of the remaining leaf As around the stalk, then add Bs, Cs, Ds and Es. Prepare your chosen container and insert the cabbage following the weighted method on page 15.

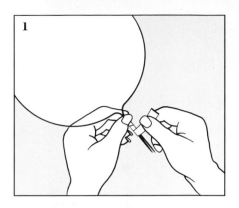

1 Bend thick wire into a circle; bend the ends downwards and tape together with masking tape. Fill your container with quick-set cement using the weighted method on page 15 and inserting the circle ends before the cement has set. Leave the cement to harden. Glue moss on top. Use the templates on page 97 to cut 1 large and 4 small jasmine leaves from green paper for each leaf spray.

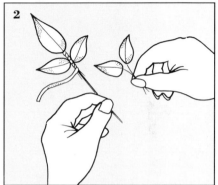

2 Apply the large leaf to an 11 cm (4$^1/_2$ in) length of green covered wire and the small leaves to 8 cm (3$^1/_4$ in) lengths of green covered wire. Tape small leaves in pairs to the wire of the large leaf 1.2 cm ($^1/_2$ in) apart. Bend small leaves outwards.

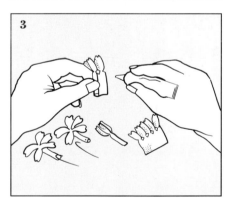

3 To make a spray of flowers, use the template on page 97 to cut 5 flowers from soft, white paper, cutting between each petal and cutting out the diamonds. Tightly roll the stem and glue the end in place. Bend the petals downwards. Pierce a hole through the end of the stem. Bend an 8 cm (3$^1/_4$ in) length of fine wire into a hook at one end and hook through the hole. Bind the flower bases and wires with floral tape. Bind the wires together at the ends with floral tape. Pull the petals over a scissors blade to coil them backwards.

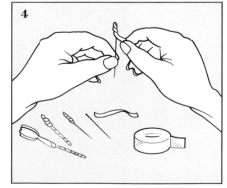

4 To make a spray of buds, make a flower as described in step 3, but do not bend or coil the petals. Bind 2.5 cm (1 in) of the end of four 8 cm (3$^1/_4$ in) lengths of fine wire with narrow strips of white paper. Continue binding the wire with floral tape. Bind the wires together at one end with floral tape. Make enough leaves, flowers and buds to cover the circle. Bind to the circle with floral tape.

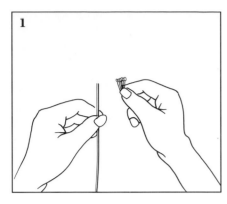

1 *For each daffodil use the templates on page 97 to cut 6 petals from soft yellow paper and 1 trumpet from yellow crepe paper, matching the arrow to the grain on the crepe paper. Gently stretch the serrated edge, overlap the short edges and glue together making a tube. Fold 3 yellow stamen strings in half and glue them to the end of a length of bonsai wire.*

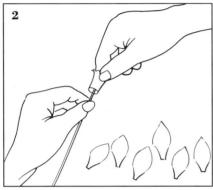

2 *Spread glue inside the trumpet along the lower edge, slip the wire inside and squeeze the glued edge around the top of the wire. Pull the petal tips over a scissors blade to curl them. Glue the petals around the trumpet. Bend the flower heads forward. Paint white tissue with ochre paint. Leave to dry, then cut 1 petal.*

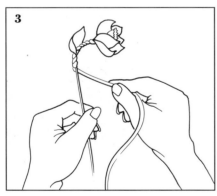

3 *Paint soft paper bright green. Leave to dry, then cut a 6 mm (¹/₄ in) wide strip. Bind the daffodil base and stem with the tape, catching in the ochre petal 2.5 cm (1 in) below the flower. Make 6 or 7 daffodils. Paint both sides of stiff paper bright green; cut daffodil leaves using the template on page 97. Apply the leaves to wire using the wired method on page 14.*

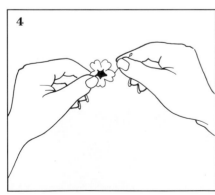

4 *Use the template on page 96 to cut primroses from yellow paper. Paint the centres with ochre paint. Pull the petals over a scissors blade to curl them backwards. Pierce a hole through the centre. Cut a yellow stamen string in half, insert one half through the hole and dab glue on the underside to secure in place. Wedge a piece of oasis in a willow ring. Glue moss on top. Insert the daffodils and leaves. Glue the primroses amongst the moss to finish the arrangement.*

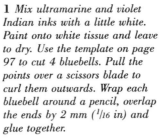

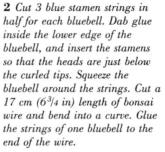

◄ *Nestle small candy eggs amongst daffodils and primroses on this Easter ring to delight a child, or simply welcome springtime with a pretty ring of bluebells and crocuses complete with hovering white butterflies.*

1 *Mix ultramarine and violet Indian inks with a little white. Paint onto white tissue and leave to dry. Use the template on page 97 to cut 4 bluebells. Pull the points over a scissors blade to curl them outwards. Wrap each bluebell around a pencil, overlap the ends by 2 mm (¹/₁₆ in) and glue together.*

2 *Cut 3 blue stamen strings in half for each bluebell. Dab glue inside the lower edge of the bluebell, and insert the stamens so that the heads are just below the curled tips. Squeeze the bluebell around the strings. Cut a 17 cm (6³/₄ in) length of bonsai wire and bend into a curve. Glue the strings of one bluebell to the end of the wire.*

3 *Cut 4 slivers of painted paper 2.5 cm (1 in) long. Bind the base of a bluebell to the wire with floral tape, catching in 1 sliver of paper on top of the wire 6 mm (¹/₄ in) from the bluebell. Continue binding the wire, adding the remaining bluebells 1.5 cm (⁵/₈ in) apart below the wire with the slivers on top. Insert a pencil point into the flowers to open them out. Use the template on page 97 to cut 5 bluebell leaves from green paper. Pull the tips over a scissors blade to curl them. Apply to wire using the wired method on page 14.*

4 *To make a crocus, follow step 3 of the freesia instructions on page 20, curling the petals inwards. Glue the petals around the stamens. Bind the base and wire with floral tape. Use the template on page 97 to cut 2 butterflies from cream paper. Paint the butterflies with Indian inks, referring to the photograph. Fold 2 black stamen strings in half and glue under the head as antennae. Bend the wings upwards. Glue wire to the underside. Wedge oasis in a willow ring. Glue moss on top. Insert the models.*

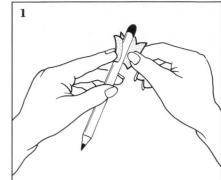

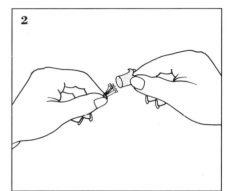

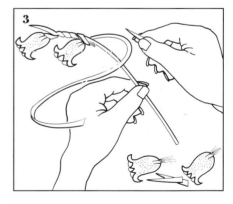

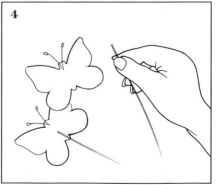

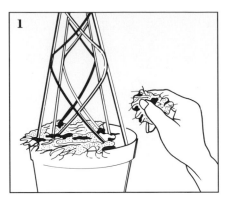

1 Fill a terracotta plant pot with quick-set cement using the weighted method on page 15, inserting a metal armature before the cement has set. Glue moss on the cement.

▶ Herald the festive season with this wonderful Christmas tree or make a gift of a spiral of variegated ivy. Shiny baubles can be added instead of berries for a glitzy effect on the tree.

2 Cut ivy leaves from watercolour paper using the templates on page 97. Referring to the photograph, paint the pale green details; highlight with dark green using watercolour paints. Varnish the leaves with polyurethane satin varnish, which will yellow the leaves. Leave to dry. Apply to green covered wire using the wired method on page 14.

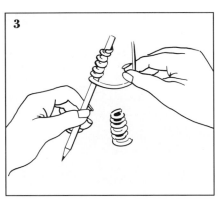

3 To make tendrils, coil green covered wire around a pencil. Remove the wire and pull the coil slightly apart. Loosely wrap a length of thick wire around the armature, snipping off the excess wire at the top. Remove the wire.

4 Start to bind the wire from the lower end with floral tape. Catch in the leaves and tendrils, graduating the size of the leaves starting with the largest. Finish the end of the wire with a tendril. Dab glue on the lower end of the wire and insert amongst the moss. Wrap the ivy trail around the armature. Arrange the leaves so that the backs are not visible from the front.

1 Prepare a terracotta pot and insert 3 narrow branches together upright using the weighted method on page 15. Glue moss on the cement. Push an oasis ball onto the branches. Bind fine wire around the base of small pine cones and push into the ball.

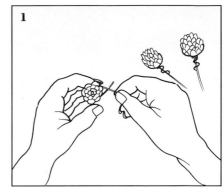

2 Cut ivy leaves from watercolour paper using the 2 smallest templates on page 97 and holly leaves from dark green paper using the template on page 98. Paint the ivy with green watercolour paints. Leave to dry. Fix the leaves to wires using the wired method on page 14. Apply gloss varnish to the leaves. Insert the leaves into the ball, adding some ivy leaves on long wires to hang down in front of the 'trunk'.

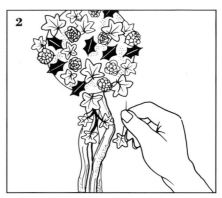

3 To make additional foliage, lightly spray green paper with gold spray paint. Cut into strips 15 x 3.5 cm (6 x 1 1/2 in) and cut a fringe along one long edge. Cut the fringe ends diagonally to make points. Bend a length of fine wire into a hook and slip between the fringes at one end. Spread glue along the long edge and bind around the wire. Gently pull fringes over a scissors blade to curl them outwards. Insert into the ball.

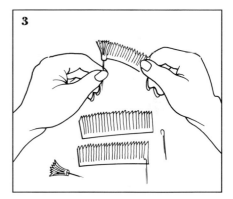

4 To make berries, dab the ends of fine wire with glue and insert into cotton pulp balls. Paint the balls with pearlized pink paint. Insert the wires into plastic clay to dry. Dab the berries with gold paint and insert the berries into the ball. Spare leaves and cones can be glued to the moss.

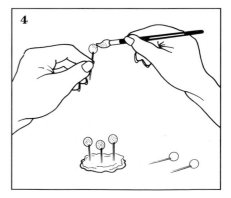

Country Harvest

Have fun making these artful models. The highly realistic fruits
and vegetables are surprisingly simple to make. Children
will delight in the tiny items and adults can surprise guests
with some colourful and unusual table decorations. You can
even frame them, then hang them up for
a real talking point.

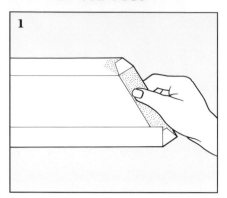

1 Use the templates on pages 98–99 to cut a barrow from thick card, 2 axle supports and 2 wheels from mounting board. Mark the axle support line on the right side of the barrow. Score the barrow along the blue lines on the right side. Fold backwards along the scored lines, forming the box shape. Glue the tabs under the opposite edges.

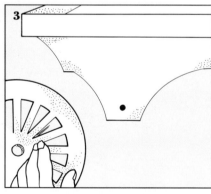

2 Cut an 8 cm (3¼ in) length of 1 cm (³/8 in) diameter balsa wood dowelling for the axle. Glue the axle centrally between the axle supports, matching the circles. Glue the axle supports under the barrow along the axle support line. Set aside to dry. Paint the barrow dark green and the wheels red using craft paints. Paint the wheel rims black. Leave to dry.

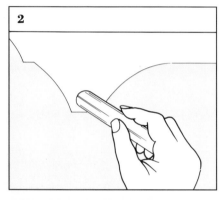

3 Push a brass map pin (available from stationers and craft suppliers) into the circle on the axle support through the axle, then pierce a hole through the centre of the wheels. Make the holes large enough to spin the wheel on the pin. Insert the pins through the wheels into the axle.

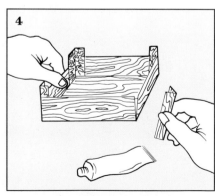

4 Apply pine wood veneer paper to both sides of thin card with spray glue. Cut 7 seed boxes and 28 box supports using the templates on page 98. Score the boxes and supports along the green lines. Fold backwards along the scored lines. Glue the supports upright inside each corner. To make oranges, paint twenty two 1 cm (³/8 in) diameter beads with orange craft paint, dabbing the paint on thickly. Beads can be pushed onto cocktail sticks for painting.

5 *To make grapefruits, paint eight 1.5 cm (⁵/8 in) diameter beads with yellow craft paints, then paint outwards from the hole with pale orange paints. To make the marrow, roll up a strip of paper and dab with glue. Insert into an oblong bead as a stalk. Paint the marrow cream, then roughly paint pale green stripes. Cut a 6 mm (¹/4 in) wide strip of sponge. Dab at dark green paint with the sponge and dab onto the stripes.*

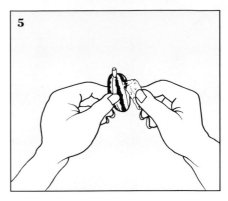

6 *To make a bunch of grapes, squeeze food film wrap into oval balls 2 cm (³/4 in) long. Pierce a hole at one end. Dab the end of a short twig with glue and insert into the hole. Dab the oval with glue and stick on polystyrene ballbearings (available from haberdashers for toy and cushion filling). Paint the 'grapes' light green. Make 4 bunches.*

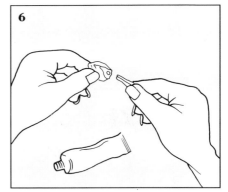

7 *To make tomatoes, dab the end of green covered wire with glue. Insert into the hole of an 8 mm (³/5 in) diameter red bead and cut to 4 mm (³/16 in) long for a stalk. With green paint using a fine paintbrush paint 5 lines outwards from the stalk as sepals. Make about 35 tomatoes.*

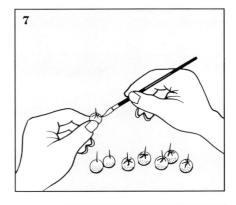

8 *Cut lots of pea pod shapes 1 cm (³/8 in) long from thin green card. Follow steps 2-6 on pages 64-65 to make 14 onions, 6 leeks and 1 cauliflower. Line the seed boxes with tissue or straw. Wrap oranges in squares of blue tissue. Wrap the marrow in white tissue. Place the marrow, cauliflower and seed boxes in the barrow. Fill the boxes with the remaining fruits and vegetables. Cut 5 rectangles of brown paper 5 x 3 cm (2 x 1¹/4 in) for paper bags. Fold widthways in half; glue together along 2 sides. Pierce a hole at a top corner, thread with yarn and tie to one handle.*

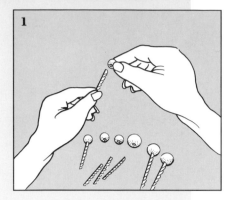

1 Cover fine wire with 6 mm (¹/₄ in) wide floral tape. Cut into 8 cm (3¹/₄ in) lengths, dab one end with glue and insert into 8 mm (⁵/₁₆ in) diameter beads and a few 6 mm (¹/₄ in) diameter beads. Mix black craft paint with a touch of red and paint most of the large beads. Insert the wires into plastic clay while the paint dries.

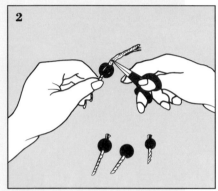

2 Paint the remaining large beads and some of the small beads with black mixed equally with red paint. Now paint the remaining small beads olive green. While the paint is still wet, dab with the wine colour. Unravel some string, dab the end with glue and insert into a bead hole. Cut the string ends 3 mm (¹/₈ in) above the bead. Trim the other beads in the same way.

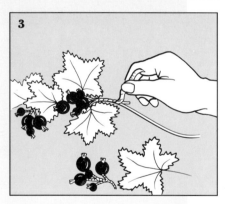

3 Use the templates on page 99 to cut large and small blackcurrant leaves. Apply to green covered wire using the wired method on page 14. Cut a length of thick wire long enough to wrap around the basket rim. Group the blackcurrants together in bunches of 4-7 and bind with the leaves to the thick wire using brown floral tape. Wrap the wire around the basket, overlap the ends and bind together. Bind to each side of the basket with floral tape.

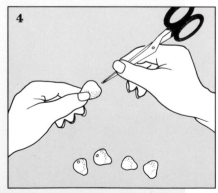

4 To make strawberries, prepare some papier mâché pulp (available from art and craft shops) following the manufacturer's instructions. Mould into strawberry shapes and pierce a hole in the top with a scissors tip. Leave to harden, then paint with red craft paint.

5 *Use the templates on page 99 to cut a set of sepals for each strawberry from green paper. Pull the tips over a scissors blade to curl them upwards. Pierce a hole in the centre and glue to the matching hole on the strawberry.*

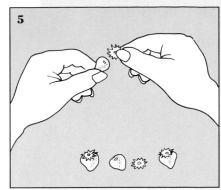

6 *Spread a 3 cm (1 1/4 in) wide strip of green paper with glue and coil tightly to make a stalk. Cut off excess paper. Dab the stalk end with glue and insert into the hole.*

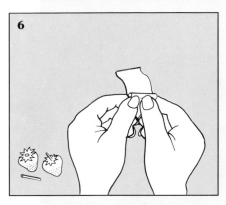

7 *To make a blackberry spray, squeeze food film wrap into oval balls 8 mm (3/5 in) to 1.5 cm (5/8 in) long. Dab with glue, then stick on polystyrene ballbearings (available at haberdashers for toy and cushion filling). Squeeze the ballbearings tightly together. Paint with craft paints, holding the models on cocktail sticks. Green and red paint can be used to suggest unripened fruits. Make raspberries in the same way, leaving a gap of ballbearings at one end.*

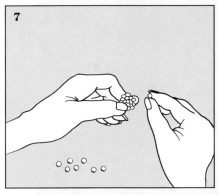

8 *Use the templates on page 99 to cut a set of sepals for each blackberry from green paper and 2 leaves. Pierce a hole through the centre of the sepals. Remove the cocktail stick. Glue the sepals to the matching holes on the blackberry. Dab the ends of green covered wires with glue and insert into the holes. Apply the leaves to wire using the wired method on page 14. Bind the blackberries and leaves to a length of thick wire with green floral tape.*

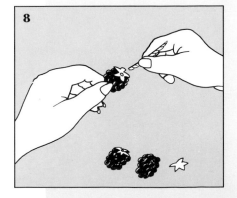

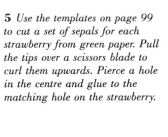

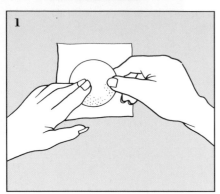

1 *To make a template for the watermelon card, fold thick paper in half and draw half an oval against the fold. Cut out. Open out flat and use as a template to cut 1 oval from pink paper. Cut a 9 cm (3¹/₂ in) circle of lemon and pale orange paper for the lemon and orange gift tags. Use spray glue to stick the oval to green card, the lemon circle to yellow card and the pale orange circle to orange card.*

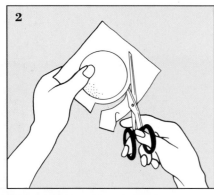

2 *Cut the card around the oval and circles leaving a 5 mm (¹/₄ in) margin. Score across the centre, then fold in half along the scored lines. Draw seeds on the watermelon with a black pen. Cut citrus fruit segment shapes from yellow and orange card and glue to the gift tags.*

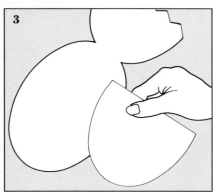

3 *To make the pineapple, use the template on page 100 to cut a pineapple and pocket from orange card and leaves from green card. Glue the pocket to the pineapple along the curved edges, being careful not to apply glue beyond 5 mm (¹/₄ in) of the outer edges. Score along the green line and fold the flap over the pocket.*

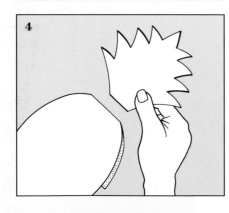

4 *Glue the leaves upright behind the foldline. Use the template on page 99 to cut the dancer from flesh coloured card. Cut the dress from mauve paper and glue to the dancer. Colour the facial features and fruit with felt pens and paint. Leave to dry. Cut a 12.5 cm (5 in) diameter circle of green card; glue centrally behind the dancer, making sure the lower edges match.*

5 *Score the dancer along the red line. Fold the tab to the underside. Open the pineapple flap and slip the dancer into the pocket. Glue the tab to the flap at the position shown.*

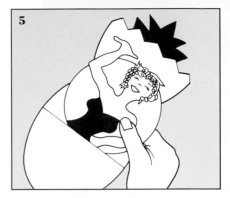

6 *To make the bunch of bananas card, cut 4 banana shapes from yellow card. Colour the ends black with a felt pen. Attach together at the black ends with a brass paper fastener.*

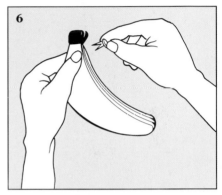

7 *To make the bunch of grapes, dab one end of 15 cm (6 in) lengths of fine green covered wire with glue and insert into 2 cm (³/4 in) diameter cotton pulp balls. Mix together equal amounts of mauve and blue paint and paint the balls. Stand in plastic clay to dry, then rub the grapes with talcum powder to give the effect of a bloom on the surface.*

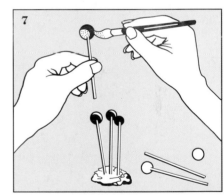

8 *Use the template on page 99 to cut 2 vine leaves from green paper. Apply to fine green covered wire following the wired method on page 14. Arrange the grapes together in a bunch. Twist the wires together to make a stalk. Add the leaves at the top of the bunch. Bind the stalk with brown floral tape.*

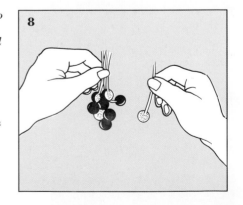

◄ *The tangy colours of tropical fruits will cheer the recipients of these greetings cards and tags. Open the pineapple to reveal a dancer from the South Seas. The bunch of grapes makes an unusual trimming to add to a celebration gift.*

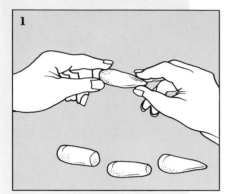

1 *To make a mould for the chillies, roll 4 sausages of plastic clay 2 cm (^{3}/$_4$ in) thick and 5.5 cm (2^1/$_4$ in) long. Pat one end to curve the cut edges. Squeeze the other end to a point. When you are happy with the shapes, smear the clay with petroleum jelly which will act as a releasing agent.*

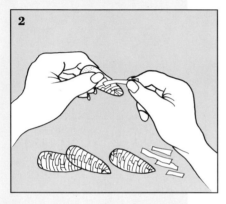

2 *Tear newspaper into strips 3 cm (1^1/$_4$ in) long and 3 mm (^{1}/$_8$ in) to 1 cm (^{3}/$_8$ in) wide. Mix PVA medium with a little water to thin it; apply to the strips with an old paintbrush. Stick the strips smoothly onto the moulds, overlapping paper edges and using the finer strips at the ends. Apply 5 layers of papier mâché. Leave to dry between layers. Using different coloured papers for each layer will help you see one layer against another.*

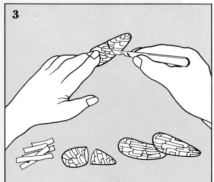

3 *To remove the mould, cut the papier mâché around the middle of the chilli and pull out the clay. Hold the cut edges together and rejoin with strips of newspaper. Apply 4 more layers of papier mâché. Pierce a hole at the wide end of the chillies. Cut four 5 cm (2 in) lengths of bonsai wire for stalks. Dab glue on one end and insert into the holes. Cut a 30 cm (12 in) length of bonsai wire for the stem.*

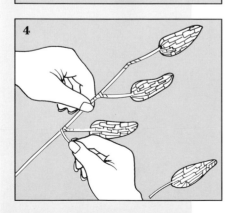

4 *Tape one stalk to the top of the stem with masking tape. Add the other stalks at 7 cm (2^3/$_4$ in) intervals. Secure the chillies to the stalks with papier mâché. Bind the wire with long torn strips of newspaper and PVA medium. If you want a smooth finish, apply some wood filler. Leave to dry, then sand to an even surface. Paint with craft paints, blending the colours together.*

1 Use the template on page 100 to cut about 34 leaves from soft pale green paper. Dampen the leaves, dab the side edges with olive green watercolour paint, then the base and tip with violet watercolour paint. Leave to dry, then paint the other side of 6 petals in the same way. Leave to dry. Pull the leaf edges over a scissors blade to curl them backwards.

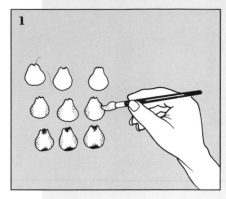

2 Set aside the 6 leaves that have been painted on both sides. Cut a 2 cm (^{3}/4 in) diameter circle of soft pale green paper. Glue to a 6.5 cm (2^1/2 in) diameter polystyrene ball. Tape 6 leaves around the circle with masking tape, overlapping the leaf edges. Glue the base of the leaves in place. Glue 3 more rows of leaves around the ball, alternating the leaf positions. Cut a slice off the lower end of the ball so that it will stand on a flat surface.

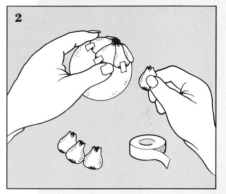

3 Cut a 5.5 cm (2^1/4 in) length of 2 cm (^{3}/4 in) diameter balsa wood dowelling for the stalk. Cut a 7 cm (2^3/4 in) square of soft pale green paper; dampen and dab one edge with violet watercolour paint. Leave to dry. Glue the square around the stalk with the violet edge at one end. Snip the other end to the stalk. Glue the snipped edge over the wood. Cut a 1.8 cm (1^1/16 in) circle of pale green paper and glue over the end.

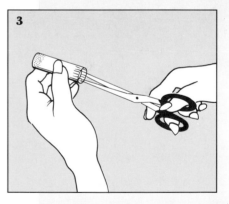

4 Glue the violet end of the stalk to the flat end of the ball. Take the 6 leaves that have been set aside and glue around the artichoke covering the stalk to ball join.

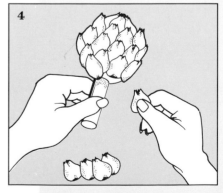

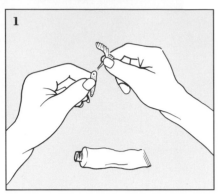

1 *To make a carrot, cut 2.2 cm (⁷/₈ in) off the end of a wooden cocktail stick. Cover with orange crepe paper, binding the crepe paper around the stick to fatten it. Pierce a hole in the end. Use the template on page 100 to cut a leaf from green paper. Dab the end with glue and insert the leaf into the hole.*

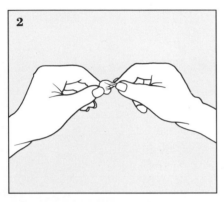

2 *To make an onion, cut a 4.8 cm (1⁷/₈ in) diameter circle of white tissue. Dab glue around the hole of a 1.2 cm (¹/₂ in) diameter pearl bead and place centrally on the tissue circle. Wrap the bead in the circle, twisting the tissue edges together. Dab the twist with glue to hold in place.*

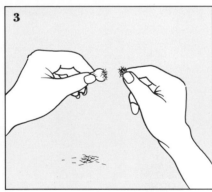

3 *Pierce a hole through the tissue under the lower hole and insert wire into the hole to hold while you paint the onion with Burnt Sienna Indian ink. Leave to dry. Remove the wire. Scrunch up a little fine straw or raffia and glue under the onion. Trim the ends.*

▶ *These box frame pictures of detailed miniature vegetables would look delightful on a kitchen wall.*

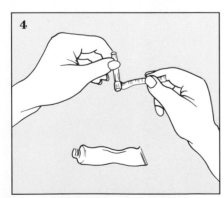

4 *To make a leek, cut a 3 cm (1¹/₄ in) length of a wooden cocktail stick. Glue a strip of white crepe paper 10 x 3 cm (4 x 1¹/₄ in) around the stick. Cut a strip of crepe paper 6 cm x 5 mm (2¹/₂ x ¹/₄ in); glue around the lower end. Use the template on page 100 to cut 3 leek leaves from crepe paper, positioning the arrow level with the grain of the crepe paper. Cut the slits.*

5 *Glue the leaves around the leek, overlapping the edges and sticking the straight ends under the bulbous end of the leek. To paint the leek, insert a pin into the base and dampen the leek with a paintbrush. Dab apple green Indian ink onto the leaf tips, allowing the paint to run downwards.*

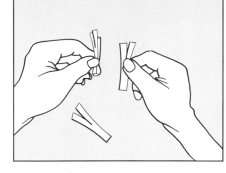

6 *To make a cauliflower, scrunch up white paper and glue over one half of a 1.5 cm (^{5}/8 in) diameter cotton pulp ball or bead. Paint with white Indian ink. Use the template on page 100 to cut 10 leaves from textured green paper. Glue 5 leaves around the 'flower', overlapping the leaf edges. Pull the remaining leaves over a scissors blade to curl them outwards. Glue to the cauliflower.*

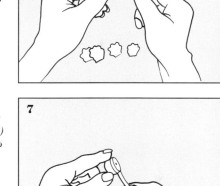

7 *To make a turnip, sand the holed ends of a 1.5 cm (^{5}/8 in) diameter white wooden bead to flatten them. Glue a narrow strip of white crepe paper around the turnip to make it fatter. Cut crepe paper 6.5 x 2.5 cm (2^1/2 x 1 in), cutting the ends level with the paper grain. Glue around the bead, pushing excess paper into the holes.*

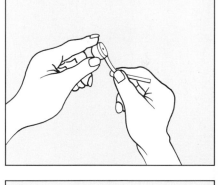

8 *Roll a long strip of crepe paper lengthways, dab an end with glue and insert into a hole as a root. Bend into a curve. Dampen the turnip and dab vermilion Indian ink around the other hole. Dampen light green textured paper and dab emerald Indian ink on one half of the paper. Leave to dry, then use the template on page 100 to cut a turnip leaf. Fold along the vein. Dab the end with glue and insert into the hole. Glue to a background paper and place inside a box frame.*

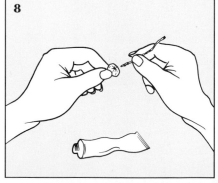

Flowering Passions

Flowers are often given as tokens of love and friendship.
Here is a wealth of delightful gifts and keepsakes to mark special
occasions, from Valentine's Day to wedding anniversaries
and memorable birthdays. Make an extra special wrapping
for your gift to give it an individual touch, and make the
recipient feel really cherished.

1

2

3

1 Cut oasis to fit a basket, and glue inside. Make full red roses following the instructions on page 16, steps 1-4.

2 Insert the roses inside the outer edge to form a foundation layer.

3 Insert the lavender upright in the space in the centre of the basket.

▲ Here is a fragrant basket of everlasting roses and fresh lavender.

▶ This romantic heart of red roses pierced by a golden arrow must be the ultimate Valentine message.

1 *Draw a heart 26 cm (10¹/₄ in) in height on paper. Use as a template to bend a length of thick wire into the heart shape. Overlap the wire ends and tape together with masking tape.*

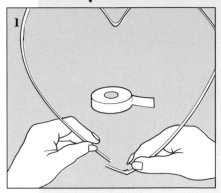

2 *Make 15 full roses from soft red paper following the instructions on page 16, steps 1-4. Use the template on page 92 to make 17 full rose leaves from dark green paper using the wired method on page 14. Bind the roses and leaves to the heart with floral tape.*

3 *To make the arrow, paint a 43 cm (17 in) length of wood dowelling gold. Use the templates on pages 100-101 to cut an arrow head and flight from gold card. Score the back of the pieces along the lines and bend forwards along the scored lines. Open the pieces out flat.*

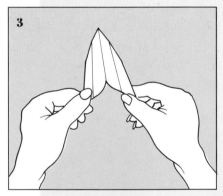

4 *Glue the arrow head and flight to the ends of the dowelling. Tape the arrow diagonally to the back of the heart with floral tape.*

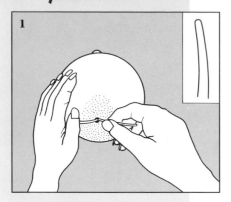

1 *Bend a length of thick wire in half to resemble a hairpin. Push the ends through the centre of an oasis ball until the loop emerges at the top of the ball. Splay the wire ends open under the ball. Thread ribbon through the loop, and knot the free ends together. Tie a ribbon bow around the hanging ribbon.*

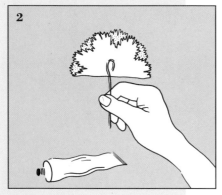

2 *Use the templates on page 101 to cut 4 pale pink tissue large carnations and 4 bright pink small carnations. Dampen each piece with a paintbrush. Leave to dry. Fold 1 carnation in half so that the petals lie alternately. Bend the end of a length of thick wire into a hook, dab the end with glue and place centrally on the carnation. Wrap the carnation around the hook.*

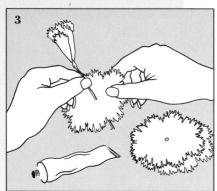

3 *Pierce a hole through the centre of the remaining carnations. Dab glue around the hole, then insert the wire through each hole and push the carnation pieces up against the first carnation. Bind the base of the flower and stem with floral tape.*

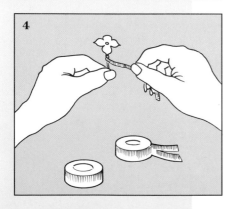

4 *Use the template on page 104 to draw hydrangea florets on watercolour paper. Paint the florets pale pink with watercolour paint, blending to red or mauve at the tips. Cut out when dry, then pull the petals over a scissors blade to curl them. Pierce a hole through the centre, cut a stamen string in half and insert one half through the hole. Hold against a length of thick wire and bind together with floral tape.*

▶ *A pretty ball of mixed flowers makes a delightful table decoration for a celebratory party.*

▼ *This circlet of peonies and sweet william adds a finishing touch to a glass bowl of fragrant pot pourri.*

5 *Make peonies, freesias and full roses following the instructions on pages 16, 18 and 20–21, making only the flowers of the freesias and omitting the rose leaves. Use the template on page 104 to cut ficus variegata leaves from cream paper. Paint the centres green. Cut large honeysuckle leaves from green paper using the template on page 90. Apply to wires using the wired method on page 14. Insert the flowers and leaves into the ball.*

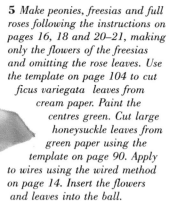

6 *To make the circlet, bend thick wire into a circle to fit the top of your bowl, overlap the ends and tape together with masking tape. Refer to the instructions on page18 to make peonies, making the sepals from tissue paper. Use the templates on pages 95 and 101 to cut peony leaves from dark green paper and sweet william leaves from bright green paper. Apply to wire following the wired method on page 14, folding along the centre of the peony leaves only.*

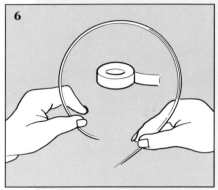

7 *To make a sweet william spray, use the template on page 101 to cut 5 flowers from magenta paper. Pierce a hole through the centre. Draw the zig-zag markings with a mauve felt pen. Cut a pink stamen string in half, and insert the ends through the hole. Dab glue around the hole on the underside.*

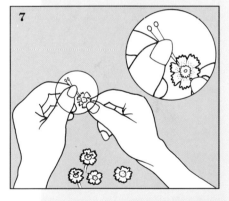

8 *Bind the stamen strings with 5 mm (¹/4 in) wide floral tape. Hold a 7.5 cm (3 in) length of fine wire against the strings of one flower and bind together with floral tape. Bind the other flowers to the end of the wire. Add 2 leaves below the flowers. Make enough flowers to fill the ring, then bind to the ring with floral tape*

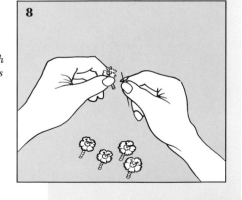

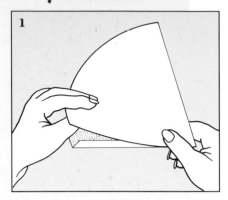

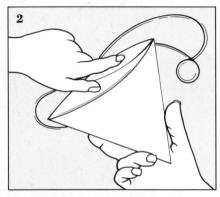

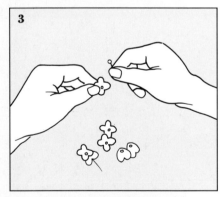

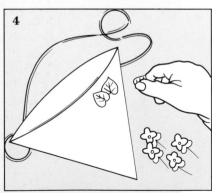

1 *To make the golden pouch trimmed with violets, use the template on page 102 to cut 2 pouches from gold embossed card. Score along the blue line on the wrong side. On one pouch, punch holes and score along the red lines on the wrong side. Fold the tabs forward along the scored lines. On the other pouch, cut the tabs off and discard them. Stick the pouches together with double-sided tape on the tabs.*

2 *Thread gold cord through the holes and knot the ends inside. To close the pouch, hold the sides between a thumb and finger and gently squeeze the pouch open. Press down one ellipse, then the other one.*

3 *Apply 2 layers of mauve tissue together with spray glue, then use the templates on page 101 to cut 1 upper and 1 lower violet petal for each flower. Pierce a hole at the circles. Cut a yellow stamen string in half. Insert one half through the upper petal hole, dab glue on the underside, then thread on the lower petal. Make 5 flowers.*

4 *Cut violet leaves from green paper using the template on page 101. Fold along the veins. Arrange the flowers and leaves on the pouch and glue in place.*

▶ *Here is a range of lavish giftboxes and wrappings suitable for many special occasions. They are a delightful way to present handmade chocolates.*

1 To make the cutwork giftbox, use the template on page 103 to cut a giftbox from gold card. Cut out the cut-outs and score the wrong side along the red lines. Fold forwards along the scored lines and glue the tabs under the front and back edges. Place a gift wrapped in coloured tissue inside the box.

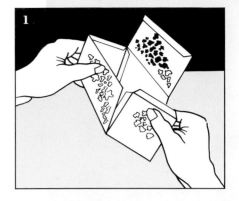

2 To make the love-lies-bleeding, cut one end of 3 pipecleaners to a point. Paint the pipecleaners dark red and set aside to dry. Use the ficus variegata template on page 104 to cut 4 leaves from green paper. Fold the leaves along the veins. Drape the love-lies-bleeding over a giftwrapped box and arrange the leaves on top. Glue in place.

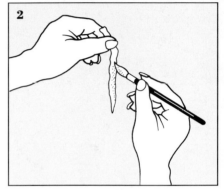

3 Use the cutwork giftbox template on page 103 from embossed card, omitting the cut-outs. Dab soft wine coloured paper with gold paint using a sponge, and make a peony with gold stamens following the instructions on page 18. Tie ribbon in a bow around the box, slipping the peony stem under the ribbon.

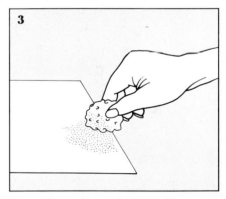

4 To decorate a present with ivy leaves, dab gold craft paint onto wine coloured paper with a sponge. Leave to dry, then use the templates on page 97 to cut ivy leaves in various sizes. Apply to gold wire following the wired method on page 14. Arrange the leaves on the present and glue in place.

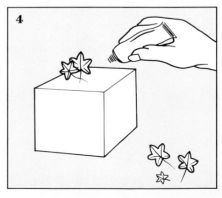

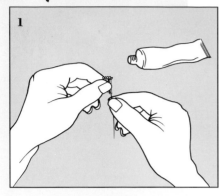

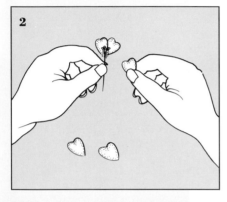

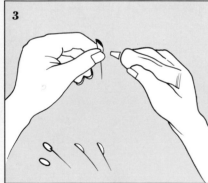

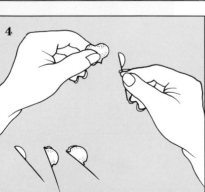

1 To make a dog rose, use the small full rose petal template on page 92 to cut 5 white tissue petals. Paint the petals with white Indian ink. Mix white and carmine Indian inks together; paint petal edges before the white paint has dried. Cut 18 yellow stamen strings in half; glue to the end of a 7 cm (2³/4 in) length of thin wire.

2 Pull the rounded petal edges over a scissors blade to curl them backwards. Glue the petals around the stamens. Bind the flower base and wire with floral tape. Splay the stamens open. To make a spray of sweet peas, use the templates on pages 102-103 to cut 4 hearts, 3 small petals and 2 large petals from pink or mauve tissue. Dampen the pieces and leave to dry.

3 Roll 4 small ovals of cotton wool; glue to 11 cm (4¹/2 in) lengths of fine wire. Fold a heart around each oval, with the point against the wire. Glue the heart edges together enclosing the cotton wool.

▶ Celebrate in style with a bottle of champagne ringed with flamboyant flowers, and glasses trimmed with an exotic Hong Kong orchid and Easter lily.

4 Glue the folded edge of 3 hearts along the centre of the small petals. Glue 2 large petals to the folded edge of the small petals along the centre. Open out the petal edges. Apply 2 layers of bright green tissue together with spray glue. Use the templates on pages 103 and 90 to cut a calyx and 2 medium honeysuckle leaves. Glue the calyx around the sweet pea, matching points. Apply the leaves to wire using the wired method on page 14. Bind the sweet pea stems with floral tape.

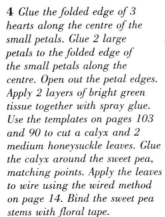

5 *Bind the bud to the end of thick wire. Continue binding the wire, adding the small flower, then the large flower and leaves. Coil fine green covered wire around a pencil to make a tendril. Pull the tendril slightly apart. Bind to the sweet pea stem. Make sprays of freesias and eucalyptus following the instructions on pages 19 and 20.*

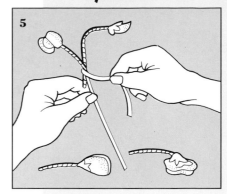

6 *To make stamens for a Hong Kong orchid and Easter lily, cut six 7 cm (2³/4 in) lengths of fine wire. Bind with narrow strips of yellow paper, binding one end thickly to make it bulbous. Bind another wire with white paper in the same way to make a pistil for the lily. Glue to bonsai wire fine wire for a circle to decorate a glass.*

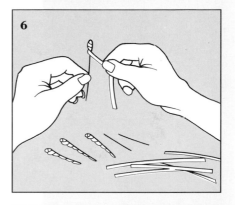

7 *Use the template on page 102 to cut an Easter lily from white paper. Pull the tips over a scissors blade to curl them. Dab glue on stamen ends. Slip inside the lily and stick to the flower base. Cut a bluebell leaf from green paper using the template on page 97. Apply to wire using the wired method on page 14. Bind the flower base and wire with floral tape, catching in the leaf. Use the template on page 103 to cut 5 Hong Kong orchid petals from white tissue. Paint with purple Indian ink. Paint the veins with white paint. Pull petal tips over a scissors blade to curl them. Glue petals around the stamens. Bind the flower base and wire with floral tape. Bend stamens to curl them. Glue to fine wire to make a circlet.*

◀ *Encircle a celebratory cake with a garland of garden flowers.*

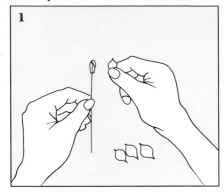

1 *Bend fine wire into a hook. Glue a 2 cm (³/4 in) diameter circle of lemon tissue over the hook. Stick 2 layers of lemon tissue together with spray adhesive; cut out 11 inner petals and 11 outer petals using the templates on page 104. Glue 3 inner petals around the centre. Coil the tip of the remaining small petals outwards by pulling the petal smoothly over the blades of a pair of closed scissors.*

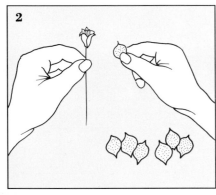

2 *Glue 4 inner petals around the centre, overlapping the petal edges. Add the remaining inner petals. Coil the sides of the outer petals by pulling the edges over scissors blades. Glue 5 petals around the flower, then add the remaining petals. Cut a set of sepals, 1 large leaf and 2 small leaves from green paper using the templates on page 104. Coil the sepal tips backwards by pulling the tips over scissors blades.*

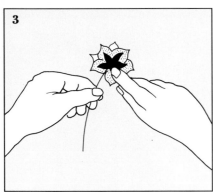

3 *Glue the sepals under the rose. Glue the leaves to green covered wire using the wired method on page 14. Make 2 roses for each flower spray. to make a bud. Bend the end of a 5 cm (2 in) length of wire into a hook. Glue a 7 mm (⁵/32 in) diameter cotton wool ball to the hook.*

▶ *Delicate miniature roses can be displayed to great effect draped around a perfume bottle or scattered on a dressing table.*

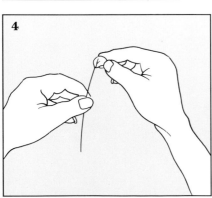

4 *Glue a 2 cm (³/4 in) diameter circle of lemon tissue over the cotton wool. Cut a set of sepals from green paper and glue around the bud. Bind the wire of 1 rose, the bud and large leaf with 6 mm (¹/4 in) wide green tape. Bind the remaining rose wire with 6 mm (¹/4 in) wide green tape. Add the other rose, then the bud, large leaf and small leaves.*

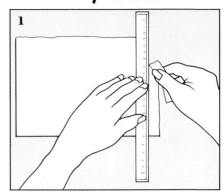

1 *Cut out flowers from giftwrap or sheets of scraps available from craft shops. For a neatly torn edge to a greetings card, cut a rectangle of thick paper larger than needed. Press a ruler along one edge, then lift each edge and pull it against the ruler to tear it. Fold the card in half. Arrange the flowers on the card front, then glue in position. A row of slits can be cut on 2 edges. Tie ribbon in a bow and thread the tails through the slits.*

2 *To make the cut-work heart card, use the template on page 104 to cut out the heart and cut-outs from coloured paper. Glue centrally to a rectangle of thick white folded paper.*

▲ *Posies of sweet-smelling herbs called tussie-mussies were often carried up until the nineteenth century to ward off plague. This tussie-mussie has sprays of camomile, forget-me-nots, coriander and chives.*

▼ *Handcrafted cards are an extra-special way of sending a heartfelt message.*

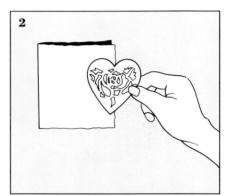

3 *Make 6 small daisies following the instructions on page 21, without the leaves. Stick 2 layers of blue tissue together and 2 of lilac tissue using spray adhesive for 3 sprays of forget-me-nots. Use the template on page 104 to cut 18 blue and 3 lilac flowers. Pierce a hole through the centres. Cut yellow stamen strings in half and insert through each hole. Dab glue around the hole on the underside. Bind strings with floral tape.*

4 *For each spray, bind 3 blue flowers to the end of a length of fine wire. Continue binding the wire, adding 4 more flowers. Use the template on page 104 to cut 12 coriander leaves from green paper. Apply to fine wire using the wired method on page 14. For each spray, apply 3 leaves close to the top of a length of thick wire with floral tape. Cut narrow slivers of green paper as chives. Bind the flowers and leaves together. Gather a length of ribbon around the bunch. Fasten securely with ribbon.*

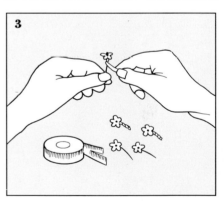

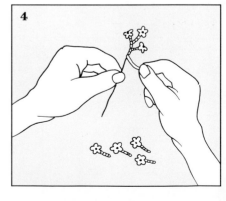

Floral Flair

Here is a choice of decorative and practical ideas for the home and inspired fashion accessories on a floral theme. Stamp your own style on your surroundings and belongings to achieve maximum impact with minimum outlay. All these ideas can be easily adapted to create your own unique look, and you can make them in colours to co-ordinate with your room's theme.

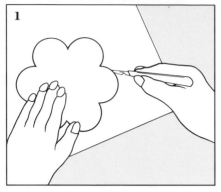

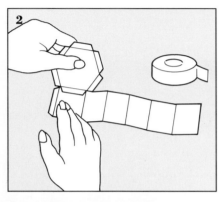

1 *The waterlily flower and box base templates on pages 104-105 can be traced and used to make a medium sized waterlily, or enlarged or reduced at 141 per cent or 71 per cent to make a large or small waterlily. When you have decided on your chosen size, use the templates to cut a waterlily from coloured card. Cut the central hole on the waterlily for the box only. Also cut a base and box side using the templates on pages 104-106 if you are making the box.*

2 *Score the wrong side of the pieces along the blue lines. Fold the tabs back and the other lines forwards. To make the box, apply double sided tape to the tabs on the right side. Starting at the tab end of the box side, stick the base tabs under the lower edge, then stick the tab on the box side under the opposite end.*

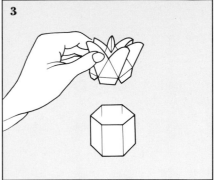

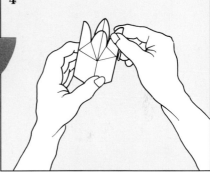

3 *To attach the waterlily to the box, stick the waterlily tabs inside the top of the box..*

4 *To close the waterlily, squeeze each 'petal' in half and fold over the next.*

◀ *These stylized waterlilies are very versatile. Make them into colourful giftboxes or slip a written message inside and use as an unusual decoration for wrapped presents.*

Floral Flair

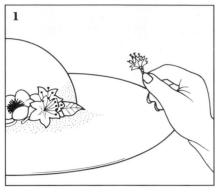

1 To trim a straw hat, follow the instructions on page 17 to make 3 field poppies, painting the seed pods with green pearlized paints and making the petals from orange tissue. Follow steps 2-3 on page 40 to make cornflowers from violet paper and steps 3-4 on page 88 to make azaleas. Cut ficus variegata leaves from light green paper using the template on page 104. Fold along the veins. Arrange the flowers and leaves on the hat brim. Glue in place.

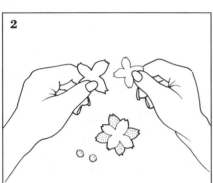

2 To decorate a pair of hair combs, use the templates on page 92 to cut 2 large and 2 small delphiniums from mauve paper. Glue the small delphiniums on the large delphiniums at the centre, alternating the petal positions. Glue a jewellery stone in the centre. Paint veins on the petals with glitter paints. Glue the flowers to the top of the hair combs.

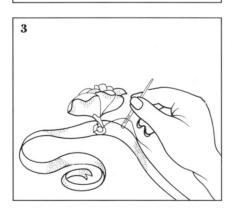

3 To make a rose choker, stick 2 layers of fine handmade paper together with spray adhesive. Follow the instructions on page 16 steps 1-4 to make a full rose, cutting the centre, small and medium petals from the double thickness paper, and the large petal from a single thickness. Bind the rose base and wire with double thickness paper. Coil the wire into a ring under the rose. Sew to a length of satin ribbon.

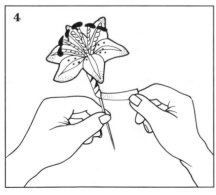

4 To make a hat pin, refer to the instructions on page 38 to make a single tiger lily flower. Cut the stem to 5 cm (2 in) long, Glue against the end of a hat pin. Bind in place with floral tape.

▶ Floral themes lend themselves splendidly to fashion accessories. Here is an exciting selection of easy-to-make creations for a variety of occasions.

1 To trim the raffia straw summer bag, thread narrow paper giftwrapping ribbon through a thick needle. Knot the thread end. To make a flower, insert the needle up through the bag from the inside. Insert the needle back through the hole that it emerged from, making a loop.

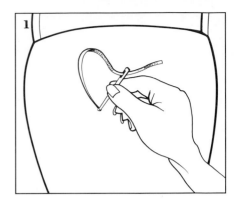

2 Now bring the needle up through the loop at its end and insert the needle back through the same hole, making a stitch over the loop to hold it in a petal shape. Start again at the first hole to make 6 petals for each flower. Make a knot at the flower centre with contrasting coloured paper ribbon.

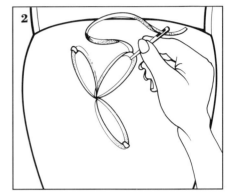

3 To make the stick-pin and earrings, use the templates on pages 94 and 93 to cut 1 cornflower and 2 small chrysanthemum leaves from mounting board, using a craft knife. Paint with pearlized craft paints; paint stamens on the cornflower and veins on the leaves. Dab the cornflower lightly with glitter paint. Glue on jewellery stones. Glue the cornflower to a stick-pin.

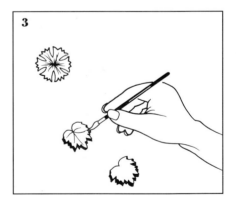

4 Pierce a hole at the upper point of the leaves. Fix gilt coloured jumprings to 4 pendant holders. Fix the pendant holders to the holes. Fix 4 pendant holders to the rings, then slip the top holders through kidney earring wires. Fix the lower holders to drop beads. Jewellery findings are available at craft shops.

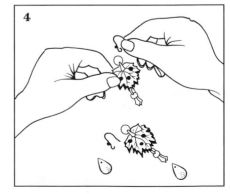

Floral Flair

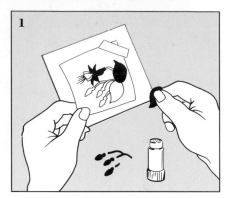

1 *Use the templates on page 107 to cut 2 irises or a fuchsia from coloured papers. Trace the template onto tracing paper. Hold the tracing in place with masking tape on a photograph mount or on coloured paper for a paperweight. Slip the pieces under the tracing, matching the drawing and stick in place with paper glue. Remove the tracing.*

▶ *Filigree cut-work flowers allow light to filter through this lampshade of thin card. A treasured photograph is enhanced by bordering it with a mount decorated with elegant cut-paper irises.*

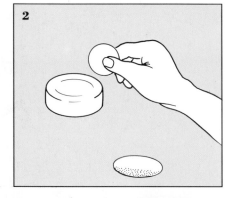

2 *Assemble the mount in a frame with the photograph or complete the paperweight following the manufacturer's instructions.*

▼ *A golden background highlights the charming fuchsia featured in this glass paperweight.*

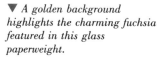

1 *To make a pattern for the lampshade, lay a conical lampshade frame on paper and tape in place at the top and bottom rim with masking tape. Wrap the paper smoothly around the frame, taping it in place occasionally. Overlap the paper where it meets. Draw around the frame above the top rim and below the bottom rim. Mark the position of the support struts and overlapped edges.*

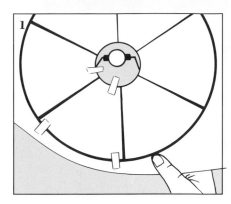

2 *Remove the pattern. Add 1.5 cm (⁵/₈ in) to one overlapping end, add 8 mm (⁵/₁₆ in) to the lower edge and 5 mm (¹/₄ in) to the top edge. Cut out the pattern and use as a template to cut the lampshade from card. Mark the position of the support struts. Refer to the templates on page 107 to cut rhododendrons, geranium wargrave flowers and leaves from scrap paper. Arrange the pieces on the lampshade 2 cm (³/₄ in) within the outer edges, making sure you keep clear of the support struts.*

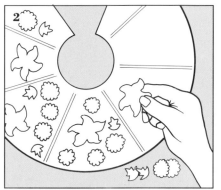

3 *When you are happy with the design, draw around the black lines of the templates. Add a few buds using the template on page 107. Cut the motifs with a craft knife along the black lines only. Pierce a hole in the geraniums with a pin.*

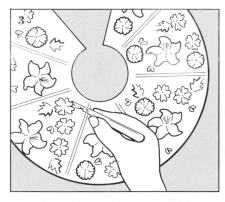

4 *Overlap the lampshade ends by 1.5 cm (⁵/₈ in) and glue together. Use a hole punch to make holes 1 cm (³/₈ in) below the top edge 2.5 cm (1 in) apart. Slip the lampshade over the frame. Lace the top edge to the top rim of the frame with cord, fastening with a bow. Dab the cut ends of the cord with glue to prevent fraying. Glue card around the lower edge. Gently coil the petal, leaf and bud edges around a pencil to curl them away from the shade.*

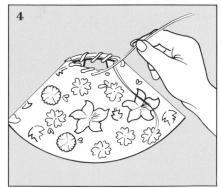

Floral Flair

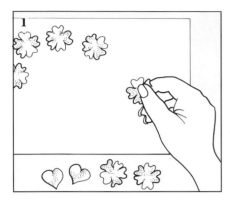

1 Cut a rectangle of paper 38.4 x 18 cm (16 x 7 in). For the pink fan, use the templates on pages 101 and 104 to cut peony sepals and hydrangea florets from coloured tissue. For the yellow fan, use the templates on pages 96 and 101 to cut primroses and violet leaves from coloured tissue. Arrange the pieces on the paper, keeping the design towards the upper edge.

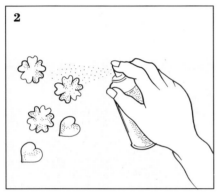

2 Stick the tissue pieces in place with spray adhesive or paper glue. Cut circles of yellow tissue; glue to the flowers as centres. Add some circles at the edge of your design if you wish.

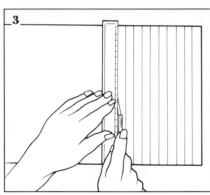

3 Turn the paper over and score lightly across the back widthways, making 1.2 cm ($^1/_2$ in) wide divisions. Fold the fan in concertina pleats along the scored lines. Pull the fan open again.

▶ Hang these sophisticated Japanese-style fans on a wall or make unusual greetings cards by writing a message on the back before they are folded.

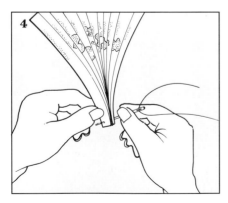

4 Thread a needle with thread. Refold the fan again along the lower edge. Insert the needle through the pleats and tie the thread ends tightly together behind the fan. Tie a tassel-ended cord around the fastened end of the fan, fastening in a bow. Dab glue on the cord at the back of the fan to hold in place.

Floral Flair

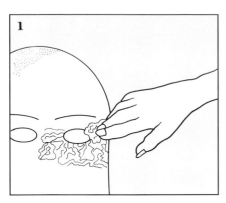

1 *Tear soft, textured paper into pieces about 5 cm (2 in) square. Spread PVA medium on a section of a white plastic mask (available from fancy dress and party shops). Press on the paper, scrunching it to fit. Trim the paper around the outer edge and stick to the underside through the eye holes.*

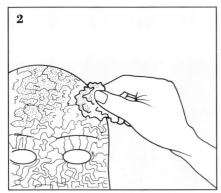

2 *Paint a thin film of paint on an old plate - pale green for the spring mask, peach for the autumn mask. Dab at the paint with a damp natural sponge. Lightly dab paint on the mask to define the mouth, eyes, cheeks and forehead. Cut ivy, peony and autumn leaves using the templates on pages 95, 97 and 107. Paint the leaves with watercolours, then paint the veins. Fold along the veins when dry, then gloss varnish. Glue the leaves to the mask.*

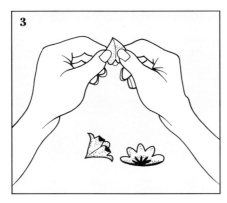

3 *To make an azalea for the spring mask, use the template on page 107 to cut 3 florets from soft pink paper. Paint veins with yellow craft paint. Leave to dry, then pull petal tips over a scissors blade to curl them backwards. Overlap the lower edges, forming a cone. Glue the overlapped edges together.*

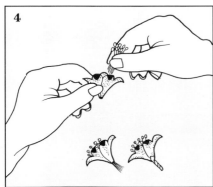

4 *Pierce a hole in the point. Cut one head off 7 yellow stamen strings. Insert through the hole with the stamens standing proud of the petals. Dab glue around the point to hold the strings in place. Bind the floret base and strings with floral tape. Bind the ends of the floret stems together in a bunch. Make 3 azaleas.*

5 *Follow the instructions on pages 18-21 to make 2 large daisies and 4 sprays of freesias. Make 8 primroses following step 4 on page 50. Arrange the flowers on the mask, holding them in place with masking tape. Glue the flowers in place. Glue some leaves upright among the flowers to finish the spring mask.*

6 *To make a Chinese lantern, use the template on page 107 to cut 5 petals from orange tissue. Dampen the petals with a paintbrush and leave to dry. Bind a 7 cm (2³/4 in) length of bonsai wire with beige floral tape. Glue the base of the petals to the top of the wire with the petals hanging downwards.*

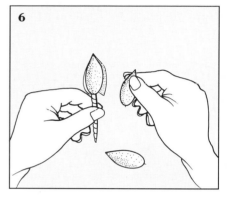

7 *Lift the petals and gently stick together by running a line of glue along the edges and pinching the edges together. Make 3 Chinese lanterns.*

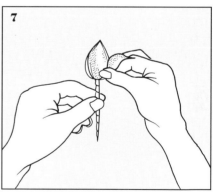

8 *Make 4 sprays of eucalyptus following the instructions on page 19. Glue the Chinese lanterns and eucalyptus to the autumn mask with some pine cones and extra leaves.*

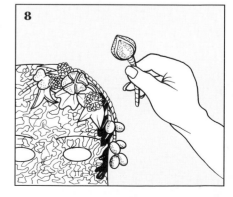

◄ *Herald the changing seasons with theatrical masks to decorate your home or to wear at a masked ball. Spring and autumn is depicted here, but a simple change of flowers will make masks for summer or winter.*

Templates

The following pages present templates for the projects. The cut-work box on page 103 is reduced in size. To enlarge, draw a grid of 1.4 cm (⁹/₁₆ in) squares. Copy the design square by square using the lines as a guide. Alternatively, enlarge on a photocopier to 141 per cent (A4 to A3).

To make a complete pattern for symmetrical shapes, place the pattern on a piece of folded paper matching the 'place to fold' line to the folded edge. Cut out and open the pattern out flat to use.

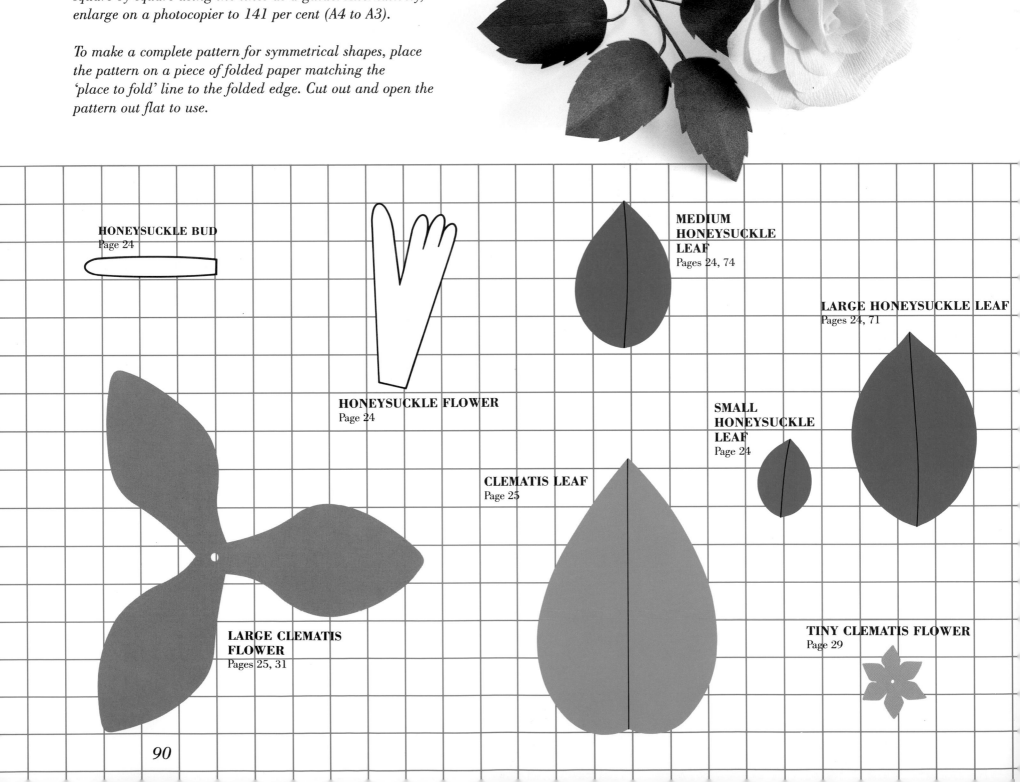

HONEYSUCKLE BUD
Page 24

HONEYSUCKLE FLOWER
Page 24

MEDIUM HONEYSUCKLE LEAF
Pages 24, 74

LARGE HONEYSUCKLE LEAF
Pages 24, 71

SMALL HONEYSUCKLE LEAF
Page 24

CLEMATIS LEAF
Page 25

LARGE CLEMATIS FLOWER
Pages 25, 31

TINY CLEMATIS FLOWER
Page 29

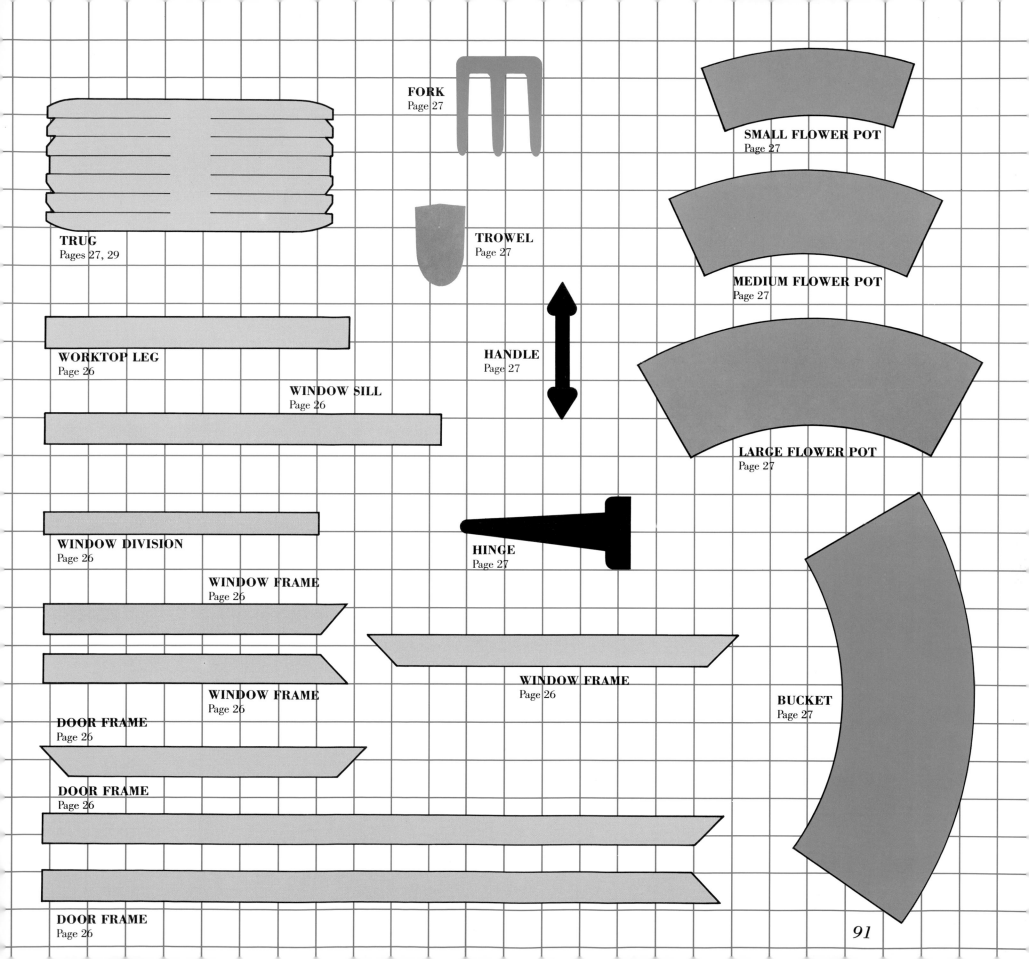

FORK
Page 27

TRUG
Pages 27, 29

TROWEL
Page 27

SMALL FLOWER POT
Page 27

MEDIUM FLOWER POT
Page 27

WORKTOP LEG
Page 26

WINDOW SILL
Page 26

HANDLE
Page 27

LARGE FLOWER POT
Page 27

WINDOW DIVISION
Page 26

HINGE
Page 27

WINDOW FRAME
Page 26

WINDOW FRAME
Page 26

WINDOW FRAME
Page 26

BUCKET
Page 27

DOOR FRAME
Page 26

DOOR FRAME
Page 26

DOOR FRAME
Page 26

91

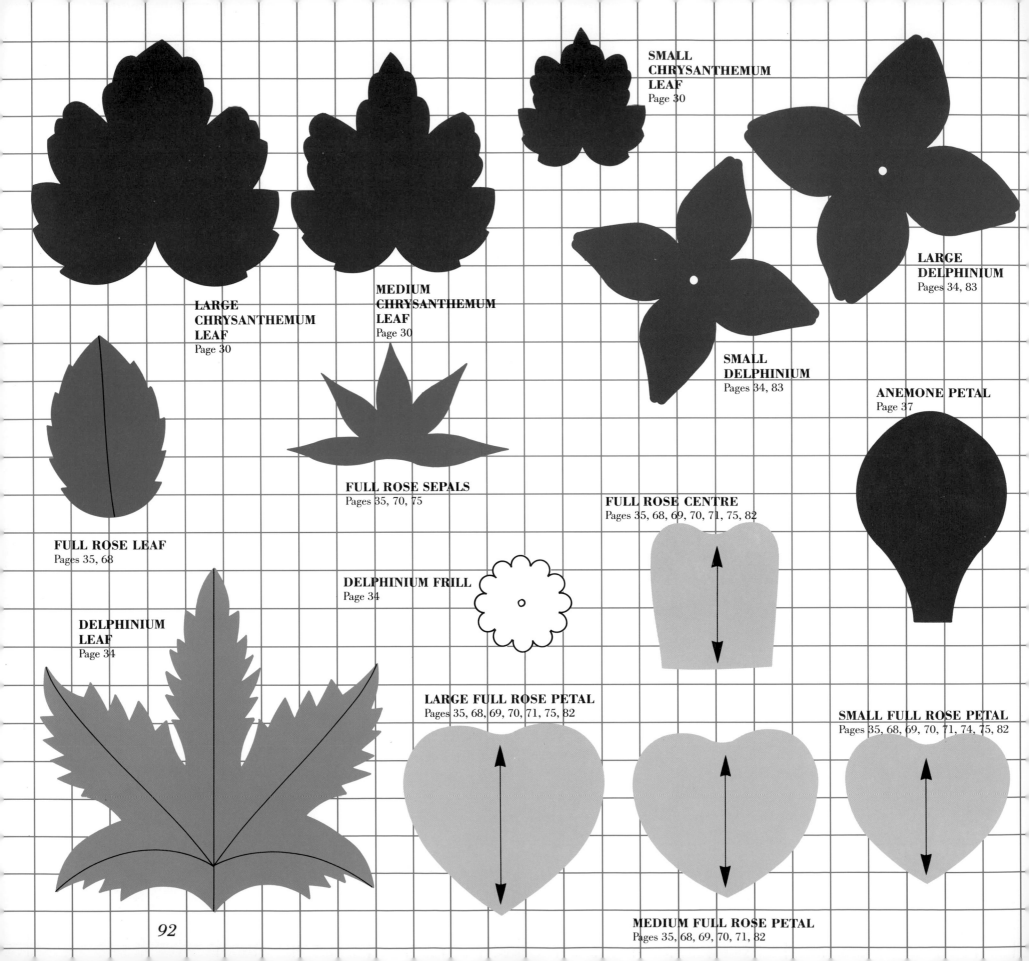

SMALL CHRYSANTHEMUM LEAF
Page 30

LARGE DELPHINIUM
Pages 34, 83

LARGE CHRYSANTHEMUM LEAF
Page 30

MEDIUM CHRYSANTHEMUM LEAF
Page 30

SMALL DELPHINIUM
Pages 34, 83

ANEMONE PETAL
Page 37

FULL ROSE SEPALS
Pages 35, 70, 75

FULL ROSE CENTRE
Pages 35, 68, 69, 70, 71, 75, 82

FULL ROSE LEAF
Pages 35, 68

DELPHINIUM FRILL
Page 34

DELPHINIUM LEAF
Page 34

LARGE FULL ROSE PETAL
Pages 35, 68, 69, 70, 71, 75, 82

SMALL FULL ROSE PETAL
Pages 35, 68, 69, 70, 71, 74, 75, 82

MEDIUM FULL ROSE PETAL
Pages 35, 68, 69, 70, 71, 82

92

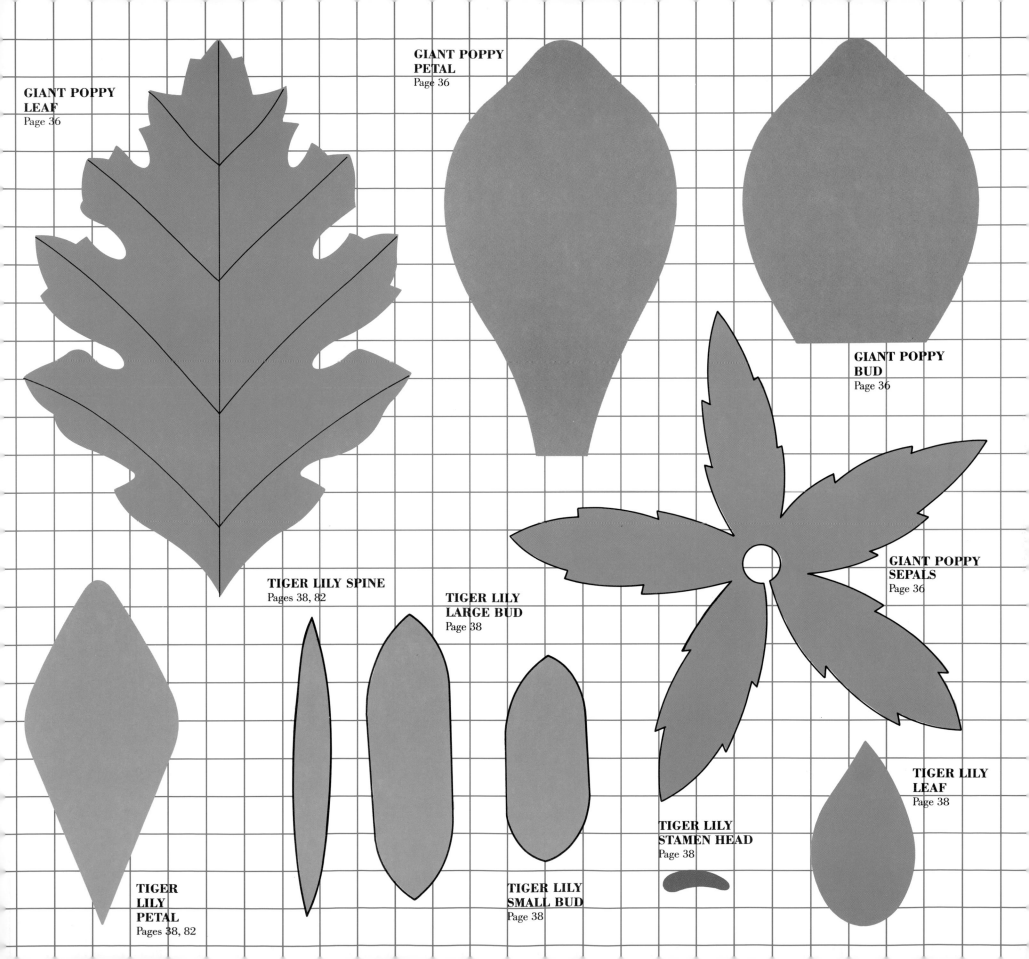

GIANT POPPY LEAF
Page 36

GIANT POPPY PETAL
Page 36

GIANT POPPY BUD
Page 36

GIANT POPPY SEPALS
Page 36

TIGER LILY SPINE
Pages 38, 82

TIGER LILY LARGE BUD
Page 38

TIGER LILY PETAL
Pages 38, 82

TIGER LILY SMALL BUD
Page 38

TIGER LILY STAMEN HEAD
Page 38

TIGER LILY LEAF
Page 38

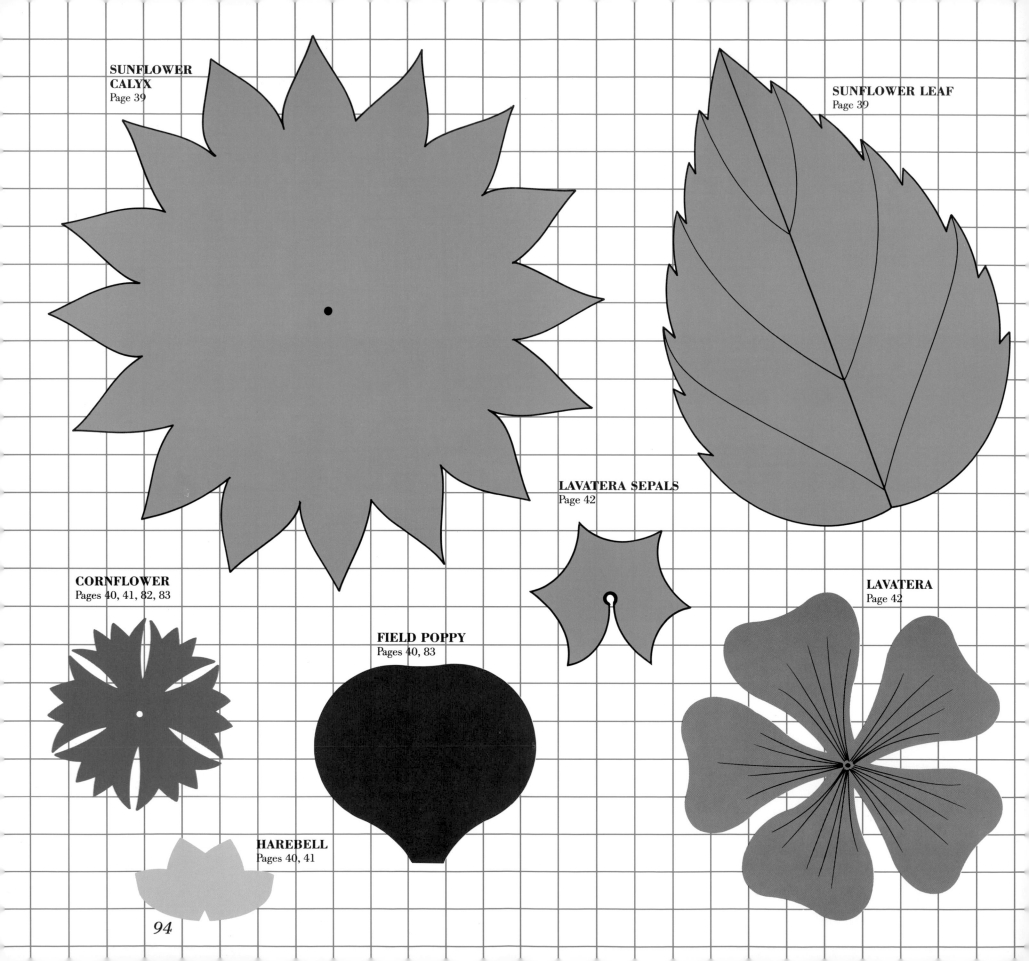

SUNFLOWER CALYX
Page 39

SUNFLOWER LEAF
Page 39

LAVATERA SEPALS
Page 42

CORNFLOWER
Pages 40, 41, 82, 83

FIELD POPPY
Pages 40, 83

LAVATERA
Page 42

HAREBELL
Pages 40, 41

94

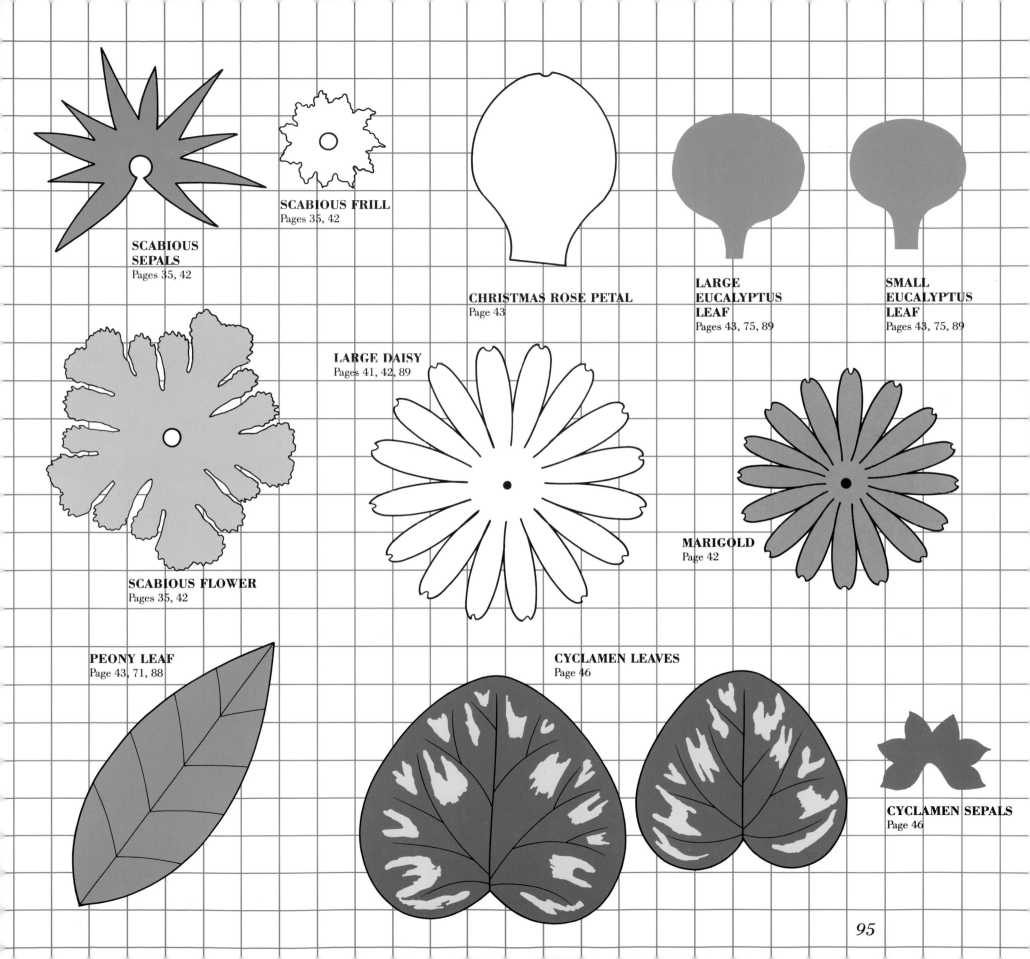

SCABIOUS FRILL
Pages 35, 42

SCABIOUS SEPALS
Pages 35, 42

CHRISTMAS ROSE PETAL
Page 43

LARGE EUCALYPTUS LEAF
Pages 43, 75, 89

SMALL EUCALYPTUS LEAF
Pages 43, 75, 89

LARGE DAISY
Pages 41, 42, 89

SCABIOUS FLOWER
Pages 35, 42

MARIGOLD
Page 42

PEONY LEAF
Page 43, 71, 88

CYCLAMEN LEAVES
Page 46

CYCLAMEN SEPALS
Page 46

95

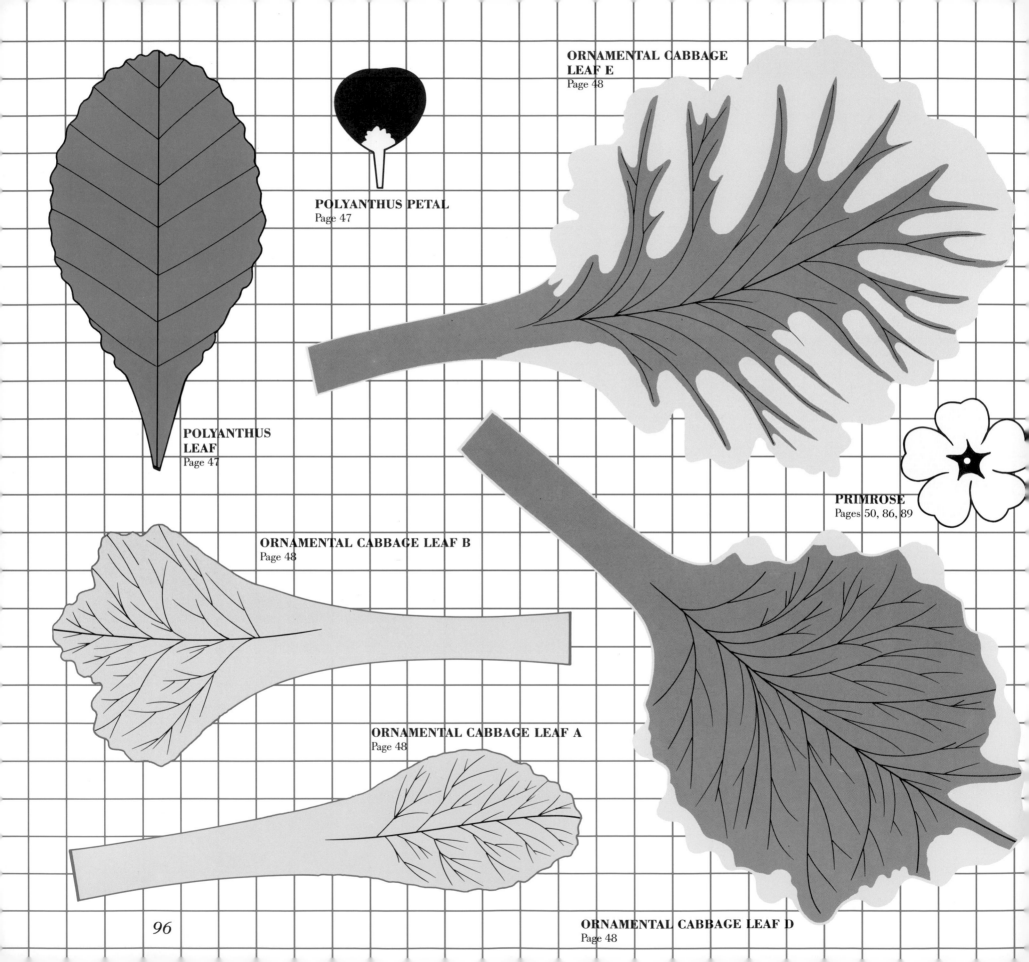

POLYANTHUS PETAL
Page 47

**ORNAMENTAL CABBAGE
LEAF E**
Page 48

**POLYANTHUS
LEAF**
Page 47

PRIMROSE
Pages 50, 86, 89

ORNAMENTAL CABBAGE LEAF B
Page 48

ORNAMENTAL CABBAGE LEAF A
Page 48

96

ORNAMENTAL CABBAGE LEAF D
Page 48

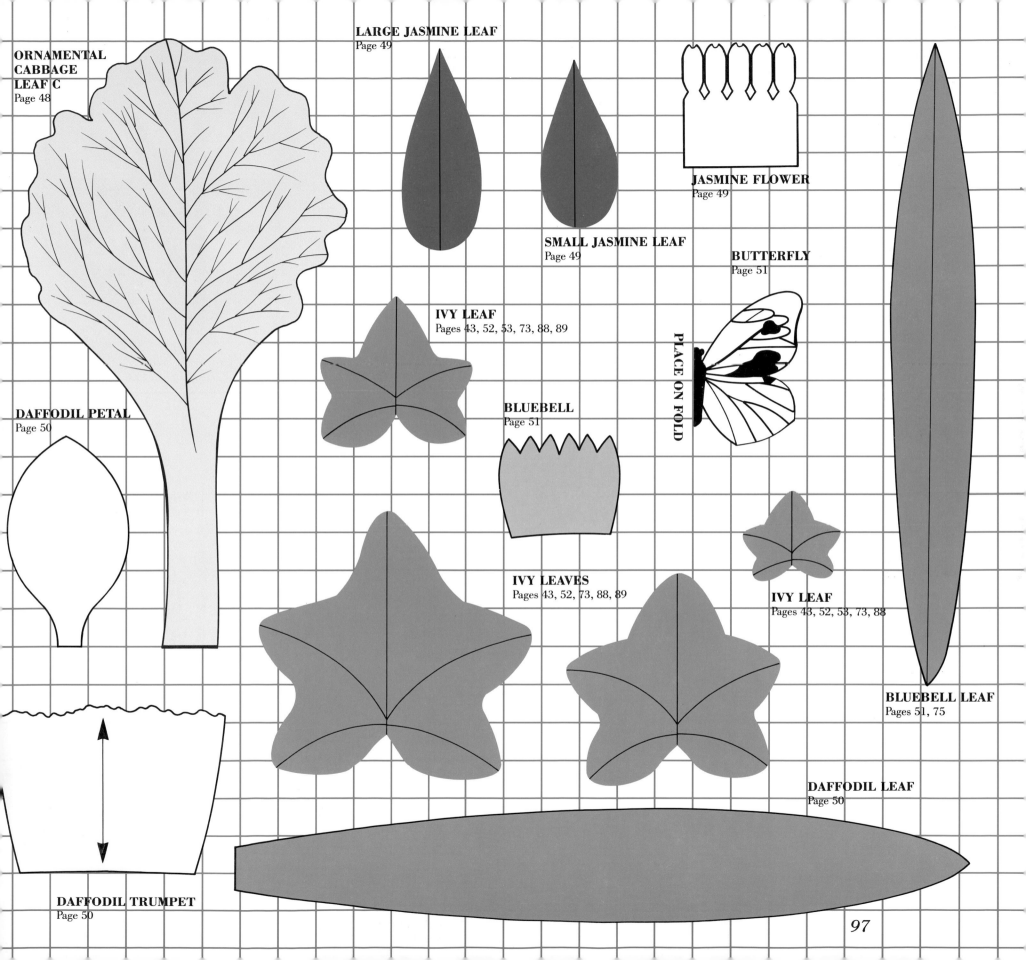

ORNAMENTAL CABBAGE LEAF C
Page 48

LARGE JASMINE LEAF
Page 49

SMALL JASMINE LEAF
Page 49

JASMINE FLOWER
Page 49

BUTTERFLY
Page 51

PLACE ON FOLD

IVY LEAF
Pages 43, 52, 53, 73, 88, 89

BLUEBELL
Page 51

DAFFODIL PETAL
Page 50

IVY LEAVES
Pages 43, 52, 73, 88, 89

IVY LEAF
Pages 43, 52, 53, 73, 88

BLUEBELL LEAF
Pages 51, 75

DAFFODIL LEAF
Page 50

DAFFODIL TRUMPET
Page 50

97

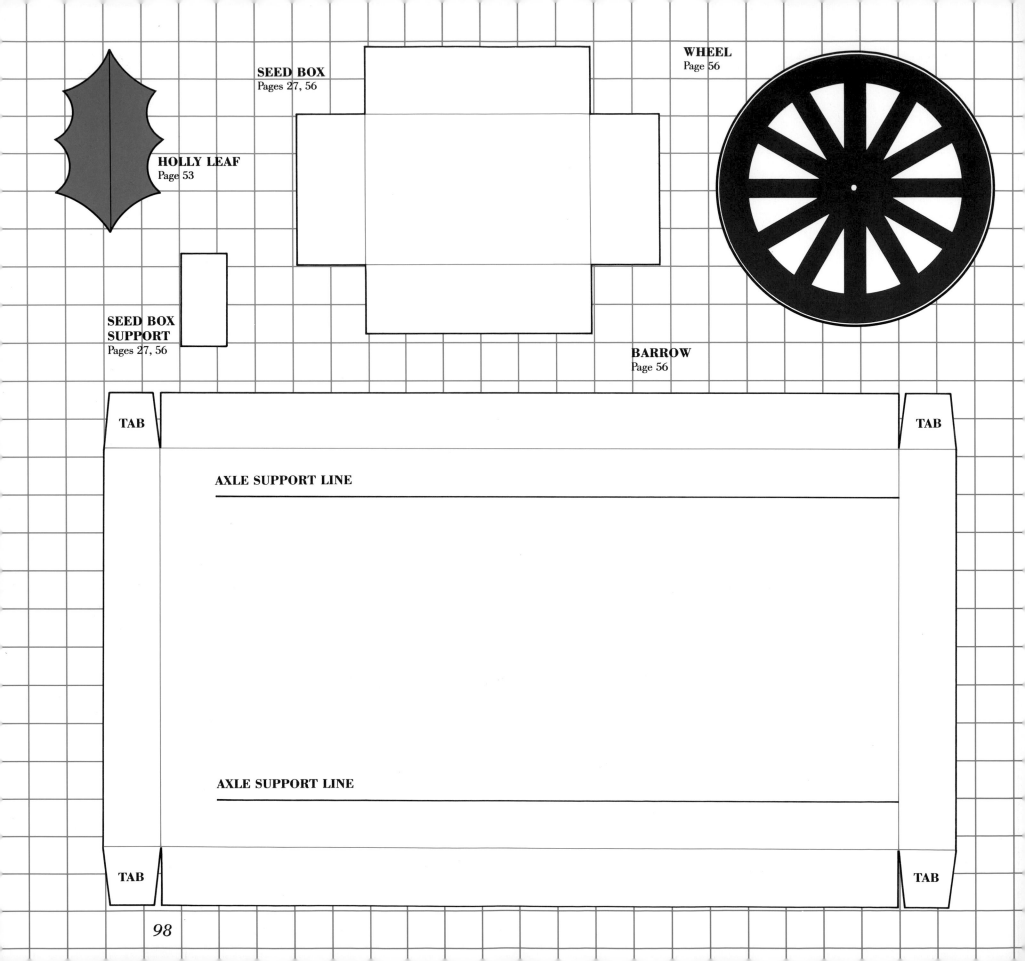

SEED BOX
Pages 27, 56

WHEEL
Page 56

HOLLY LEAF
Page 53

**SEED BOX
SUPPORT**
Pages 27, 56

BARROW
Page 56

TAB

TAB

AXLE SUPPORT LINE

AXLE SUPPORT LINE

TAB

TAB

STRAWBERRY SEPALS
Page 53

VINE LEAF
Page 61

AXLE SUPPORT
Page 56

TAB

BLACKBERRY SEPAL
Page 59

BLACKBERRY LEAF
Page 59

DANCER
Page 60

LARGE BLACKCURRANT LEAF
Page 58

SMALL BLACKCURRANT LEAF
Page 58

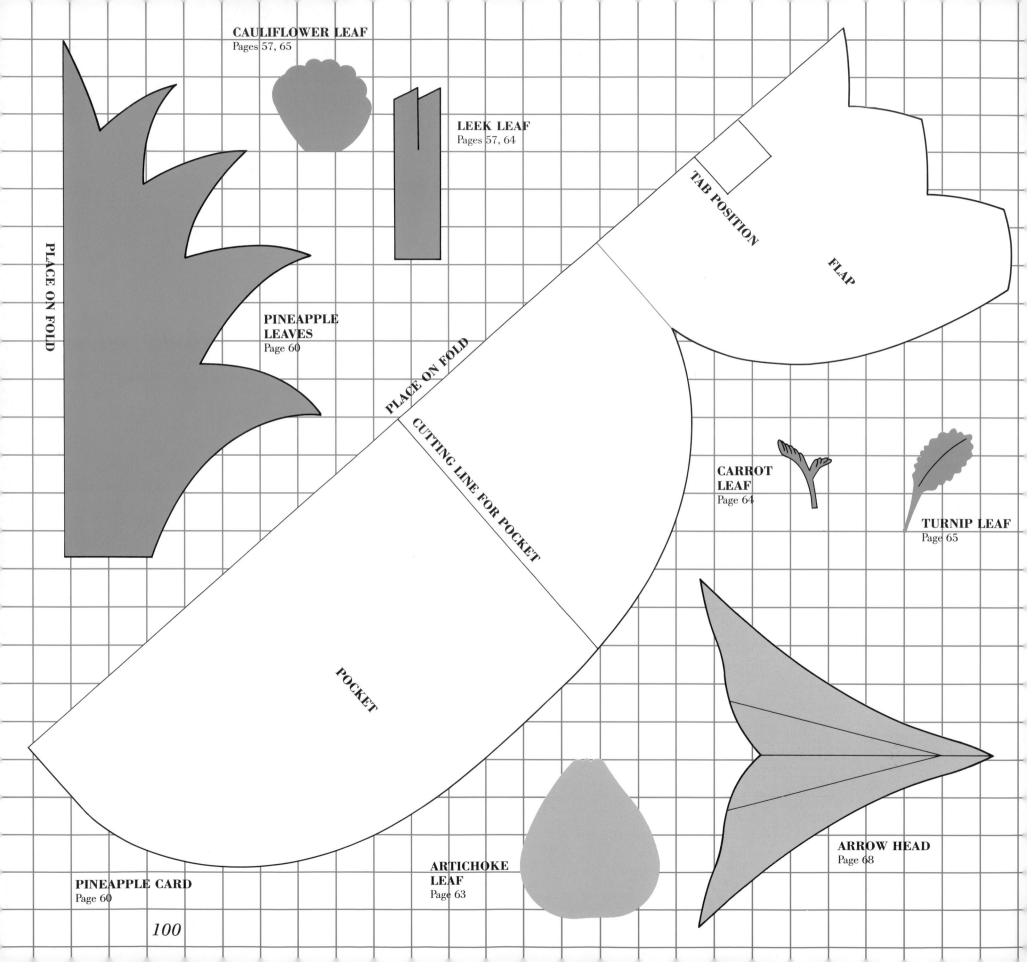

CAULIFLOWER LEAF
Pages 57, 65

LEEK LEAF
Pages 57, 64

PLACE ON FOLD

**PINEAPPLE
LEAVES**
Page 60

TAB POSITION

FLAP

PLACE ON FOLD

CUTTING LINE FOR POCKET

**CARROT
LEAF**
Page 64

TURNIP LEAF
Page 65

POCKET

PINEAPPLE CARD
Page 60

100

**ARTICHOKE
LEAF**
Page 63

ARROW HEAD
Page 68

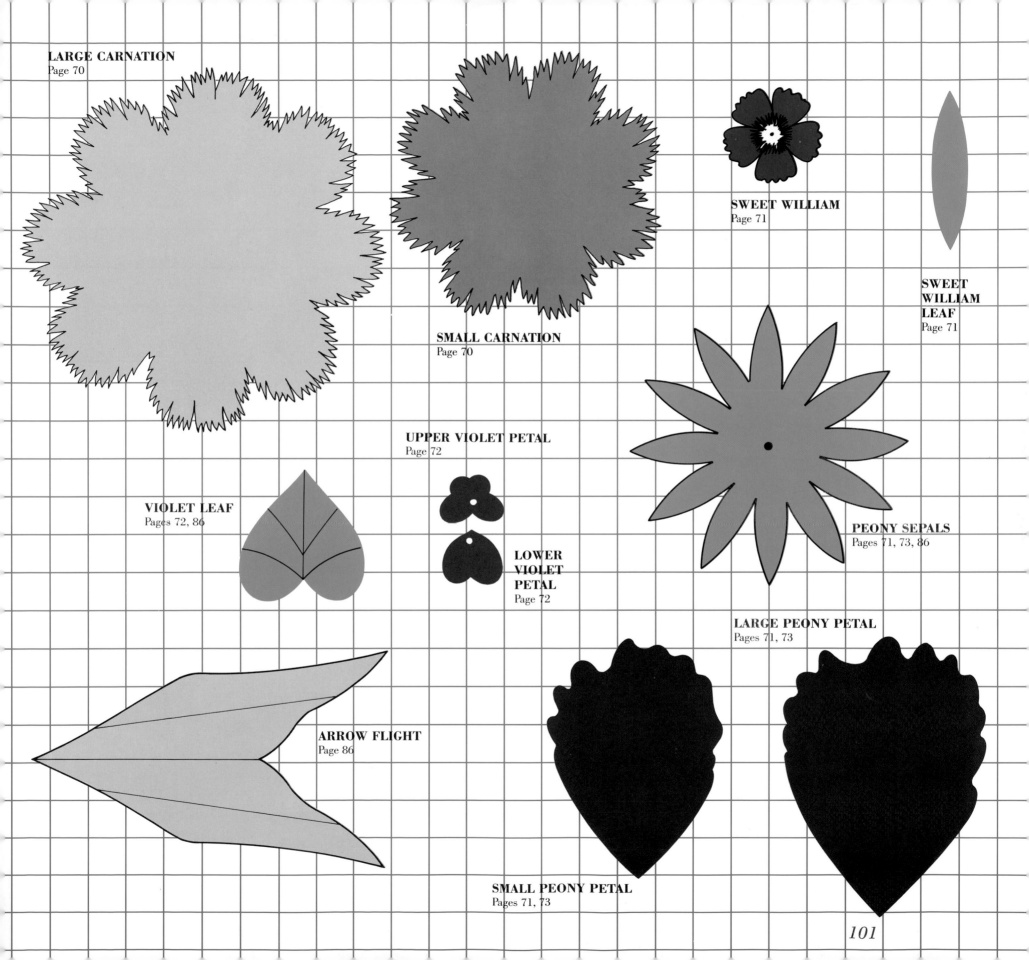

LARGE CARNATION
Page 70

SMALL CARNATION
Page 70

SWEET WILLIAM
Page 71

SWEET WILLIAM LEAF
Page 71

UPPER VIOLET PETAL
Page 72

VIOLET LEAF
Pages 72, 86

LOWER VIOLET PETAL
Page 72

PEONY SEPALS
Pages 71, 73, 86

LARGE PEONY PETAL
Pages 71, 73

ARROW FLIGHT
Page 86

SMALL PEONY PETAL
Pages 71, 73

101

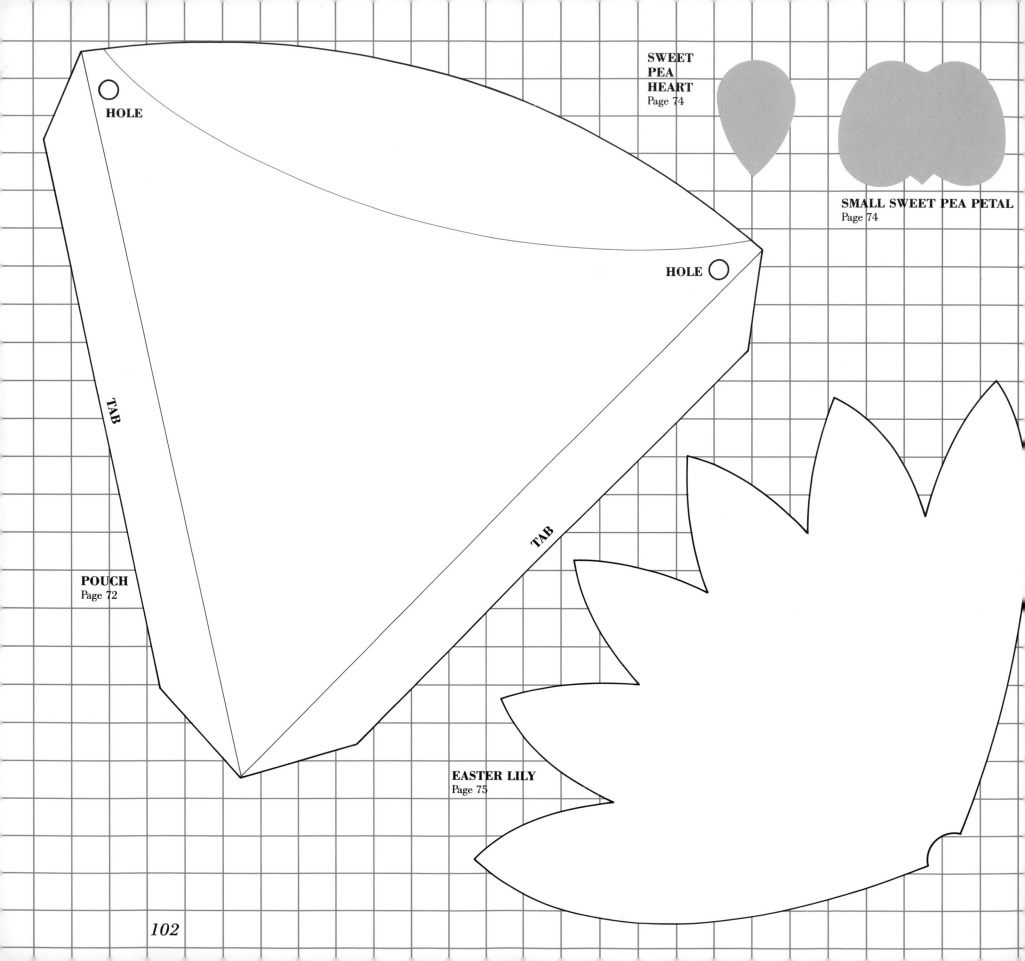

SWEET PEA HEART
Page 74

SMALL SWEET PEA PETAL
Page 74

HOLE

HOLE

TAB

TAB

POUCH
Page 72

EASTER LILY
Page 75

102

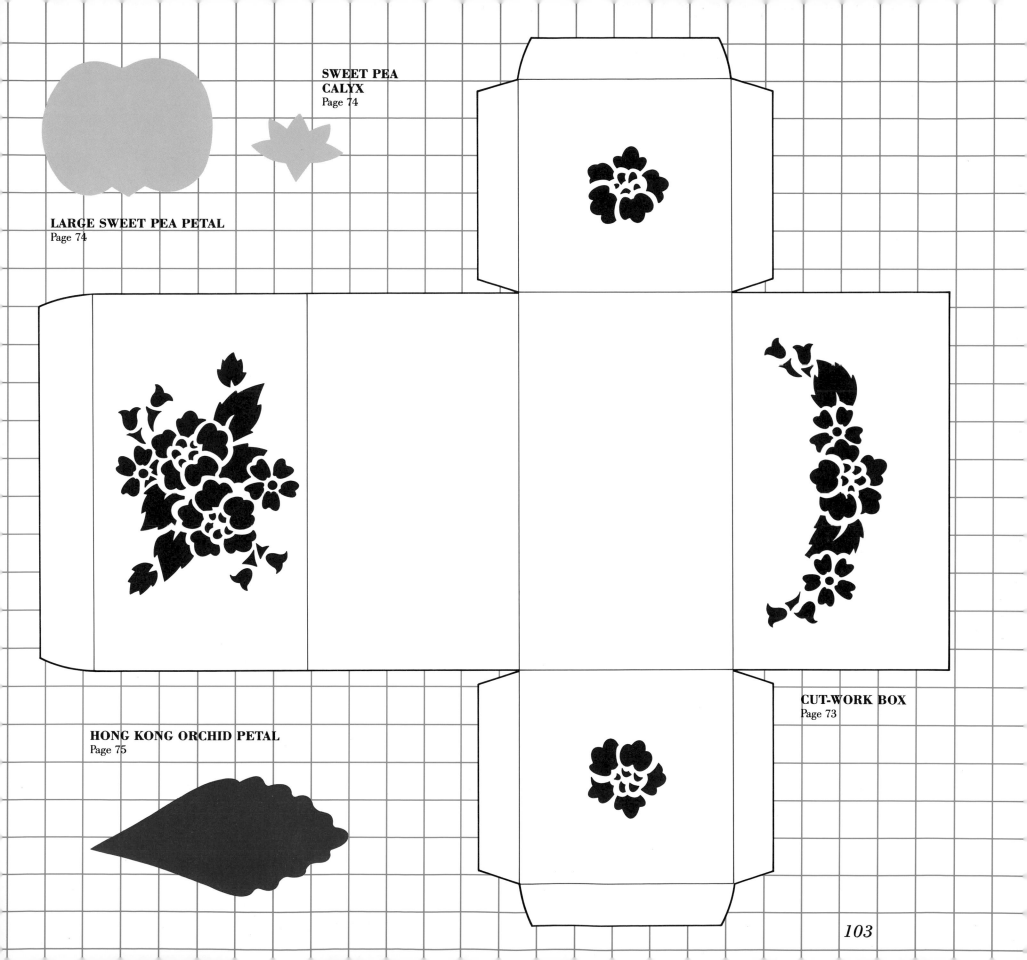

**SWEET PEA
CALYX**
Page 74

LARGE SWEET PEA PETAL
Page 74

CUT-WORK BOX
Page 73

HONG KONG ORCHID PETAL
Page 75

103

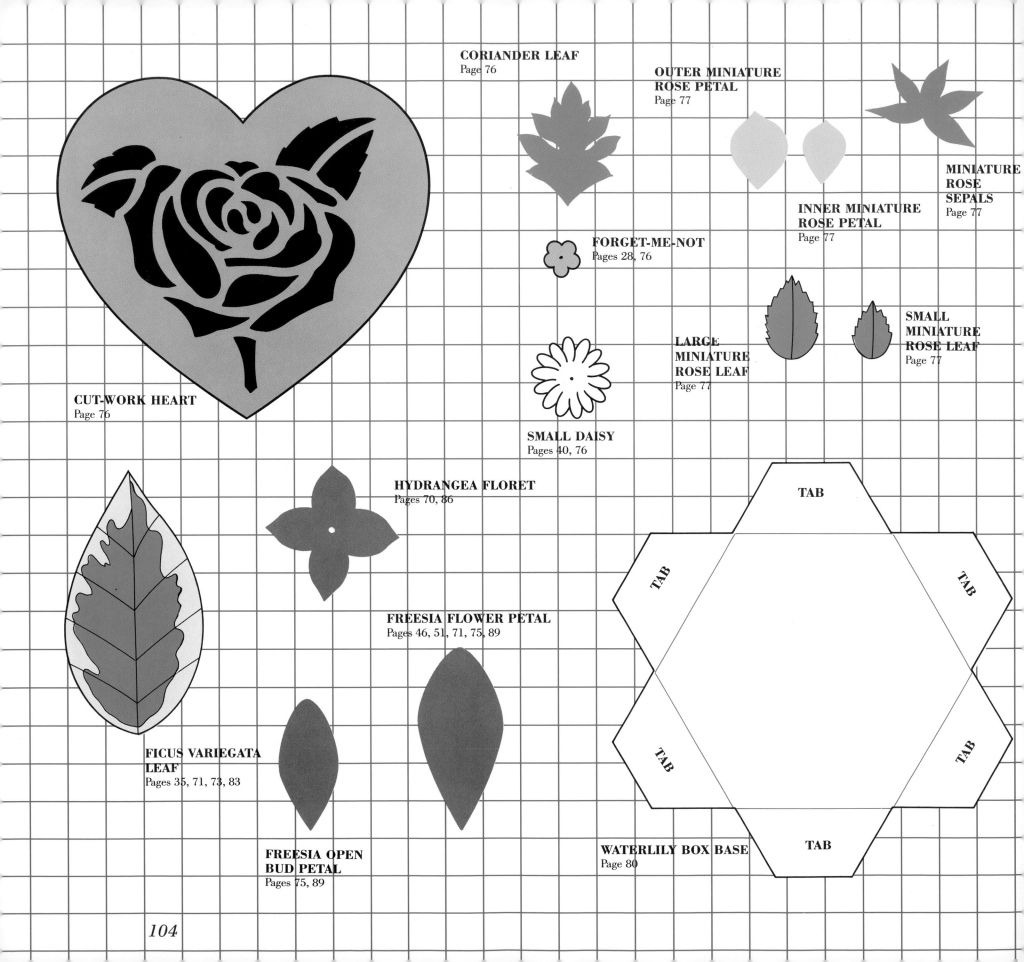

CORIANDER LEAF
Page 76

**OUTER MINIATURE
ROSE PETAL**
Page 77

**MINIATURE
ROSE
SEPALS**
Page 77

**INNER MINIATURE
ROSE PETAL**
Page 77

FORGET-ME-NOT
Pages 28, 76

**SMALL
MINIATURE
ROSE LEAF**
Page 77

**LARGE
MINIATURE
ROSE LEAF**
Page 77

CUT-WORK HEART
Page 76

SMALL DAISY
Pages 40, 76

HYDRANGEA FLORET
Pages 70, 86

FREESIA FLOWER PETAL
Pages 46, 51, 71, 75, 89

**FICUS VARIEGATA
LEAF**
Pages 35, 71, 73, 83

TAB

TAB

TAB

TAB

TAB

TAB

**FREESIA OPEN
BUD PETAL**
Pages 75, 89

WATERLILY BOX BASE
Page 80

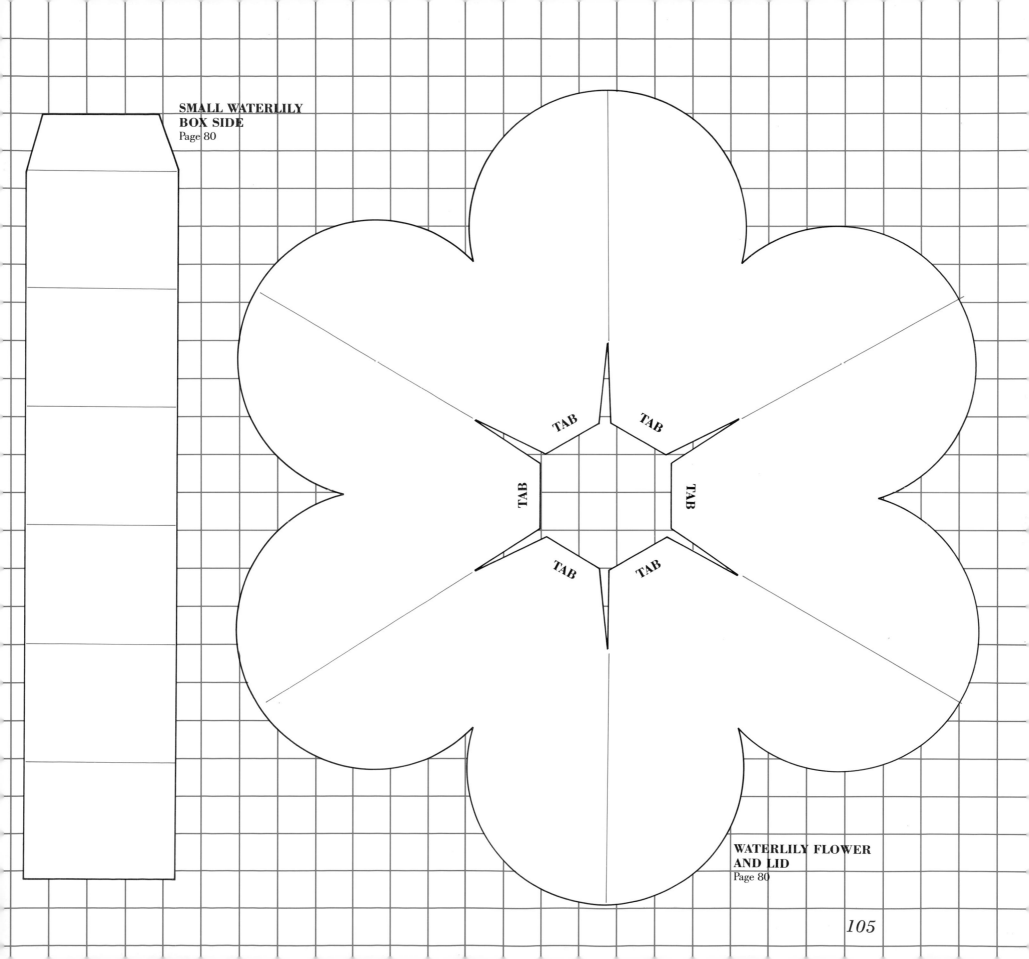

SMALL WATERLILY
BOX SIDE
Page 80

TAB

TAB

TAB

TAB

TAB

TAB

WATERLILY FLOWER
AND LID
Page 80

105

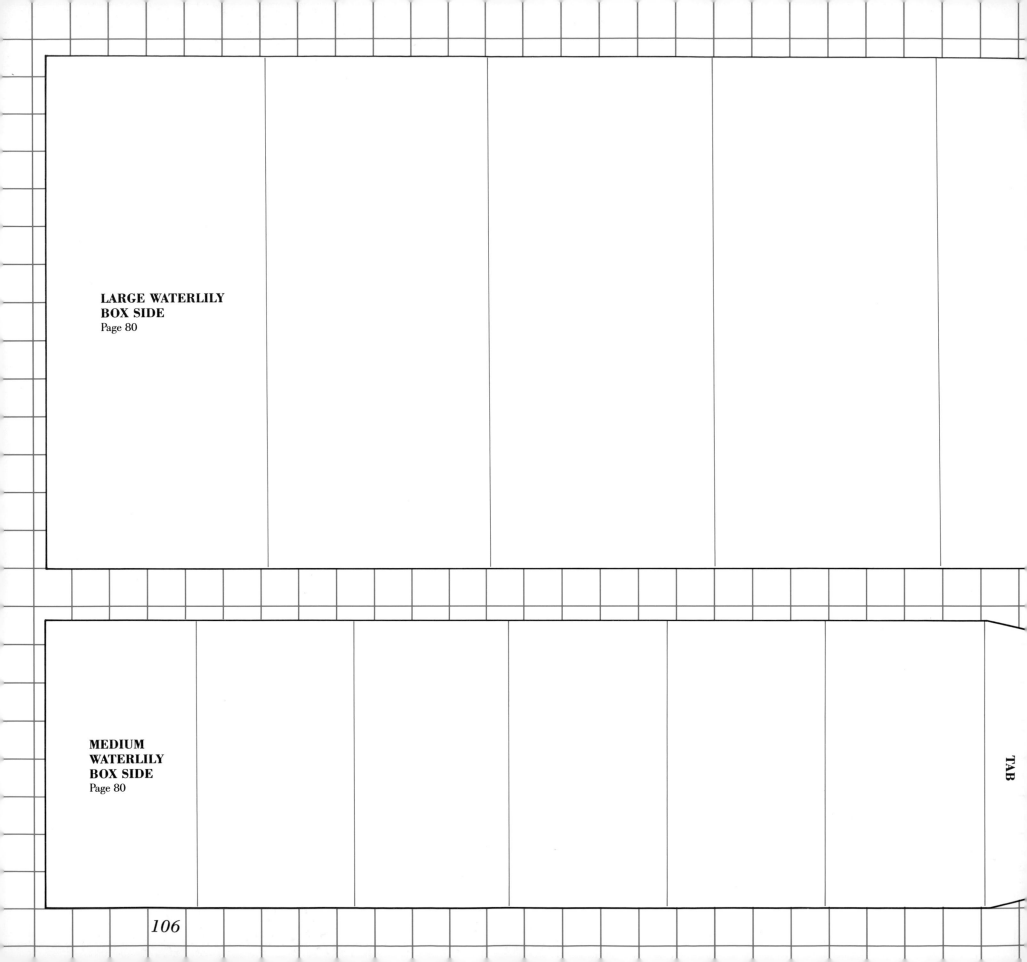

LARGE WATERLILY BOX SIDE
Page 80

MEDIUM WATERLILY BOX SIDE
Page 80

TAB

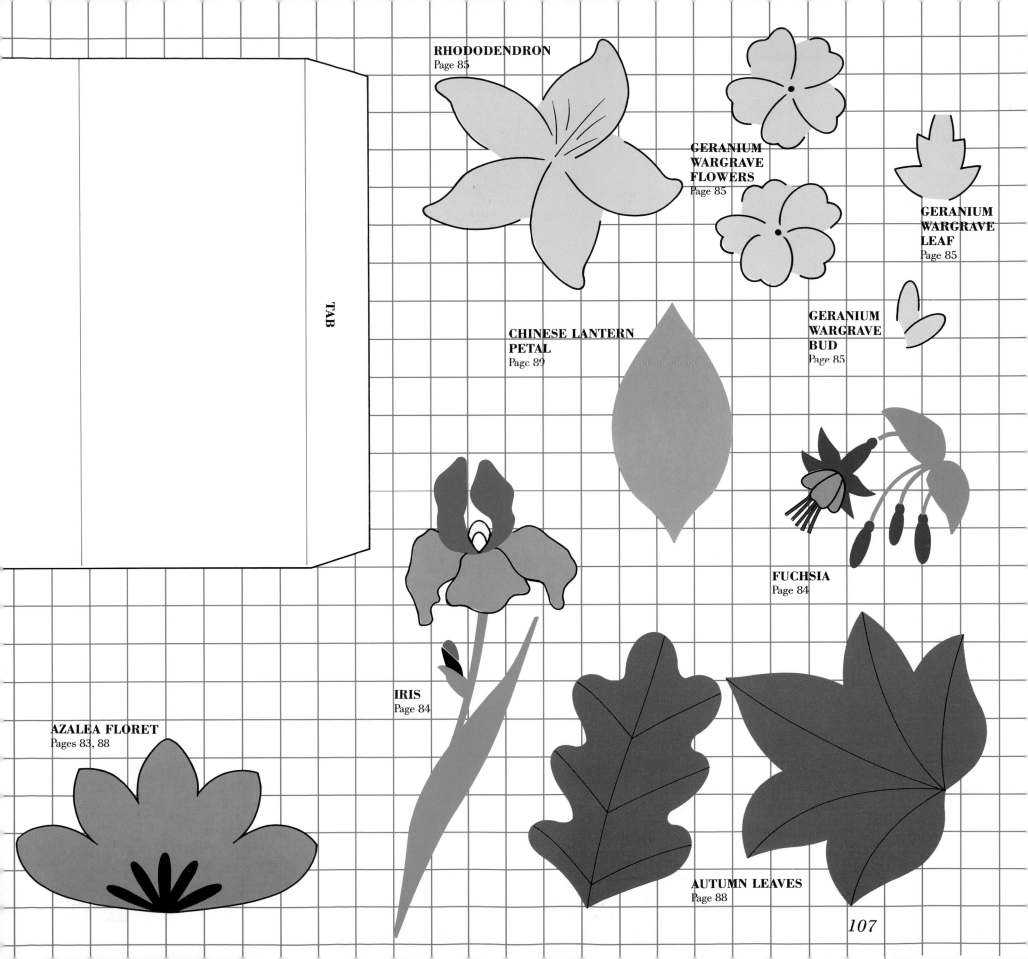

TAB

RHODODENDRON
Page 85

**GERANIUM
WARGRAVE
FLOWERS**
Page 85

**GERANIUM
WARGRAVE
LEAF**
Page 85

**CHINESE LANTERN
PETAL**
Page 89

**GERANIUM
WARGRAVE
BUD**
Page 85

FUCHSIA
Page 84

IRIS
Page 84

AZALEA FLORET
Pages 83, 88

AUTUMN LEAVES
Page 88

107

Managing Editor: Jo Finnis
Editor: Geraldine Christy
Design: Nigel Duffield
Photography: Steve Tanner
Photographic Direction: Nigel Duffield
Illustration: Phil Gorton
Typesetting: Mary Wray
Production: Ruth Arthur, Sally Connolly,
Neil Randles, Karen Staff, Jonathan Tickner
Director of Production: Gerald Hughes